THIS MOUNTAIN LIFE

The First Hundred Years of The Rucksack Club

Compiled from the pictorial archives of
The Rucksack Club and edited by John Beatty

Photo by J. E. Byrom

Published by Northern Light

Acknowledgments

This book has come to life through the work of many people. I would like to especially thank John Llewellyn and Keith Treacher, who as Club archivists have assembled the history of the Club's activities with enormous dedication; also to late members Phil Brockbank and Eric Byrom from their historical writings of the Club's first fifty years; to Ted Dance for his knowledge and recall; to the contributors, Vin Dillon, Rob Ferguson, Chris Brasher and to Mike Dent who's focus and trust oiled the clockwork at every stage; also to my son Robin for his patience and skill. We all thank John Payne for the inspiration and initiative of persuading the Club to embark on this project. Throughout the preparation of the book I have become absorbed and amazed by the exploits of our members through the decades. We have a rich legacy of achievements, friendship and spirit told through their lives; my personal thanks go to all of the Rucksack Club for access to the archives and for each individual's contributions.

John Beatty

Published 2003 Northern Light
PO Box 1575, Bamford, Hope Valley, S33 0AW.
Second Edition
ISBN 0-9546211-0-7

Copyright text © John Llewellyn, Keith Treacher, Ted Dance,
Chris Brasher, Rob Ferguson, Vin Dillon, John Beatty.

Rucksack Club archivists • John Llewellyn, Keith Treacher
Digital archive • Gordon Adshead
Design • Robin Beatty

FRANK SOLARI

Frank Solari was an enthusiastic explorer whose skill as a photographer has enriched the archives of not only the Rucksack Club, but also the Alpine Club and the Alpine Garden Society. The whole world of Mountaineering has benefited from his professional and diplomatic expertise on the original BMC Equipment Committee.

The first edition was entirely funded by a legacy from Frank Solari to the Club.

This book is dedicated to him.

CONTENTS

Castel y Gwynt.
Photo by Ken Davidson

FOREWORD

This is the story of an amazing bunch of eccentric Brits who are all members of a club which was conceived, more than a hundred years ago, in my favourite pub, the P-y-G, which is more properly known as the Pen-y-Gwryd Hotel, the home of British Mountaineering.

The conception story is told in an article entitled "The Coming-of-Age of the Club" written in 1923 by one of the co-founders, A. E. Burns. However the moment of conception was a solitary affair.

"J. H. Entwisle stopped for lunch at the P-y-G during a solitary walking tour in May 1901 and became interested in a copy of the Yorkshire Ramblers Club Journal lying on the table. It recorded their Annual Dinner and the speech of Dr Collier who lamented that no such club as the Yorkshire Ramblers existed in Manchester. Entwisle could not forget it. He talked it over with A. E. Burns and "we wondered what could be done to remove the reproach" ".

It took another year before "it was evident that in and around Manchester there resided a number of votaries of the open road and the wilds". And thus the Rucksack Club was born.

There are hundreds, maybe thousands, of mountaineering and climbing clubs in the UK and they all have members who walk in the hills, climb on the rocks and journey all over the world to remote and jagged places. But none of them specialise in extreme journeys.

Walking in the Pennines one day in the company of the Club's A team, I overheard them discussing "The Horseshoe". It was undoubtedly in Wales so I assumed it was the Snowdon Horseshoe, a fine day out. Not a bit of it: this was a weekend walk anchored on the North Wales Coast and then traversing the Carneddau, Glyders, Snowdon, Rhinogs, Cader Idris, Arans, Berwyn and a few minor ranges - about 138 miles in 4 days and three nights!

On another occasion I was lying in a hospital bed with a sore bum - having just had my piles operated on - when the Observer newspaper phoned to say they needed an article on age and stamina because Shepherd, the American astronaut aged about 44, had been recalled from a moon walk when NASA experts did not like the sound of his heart. Everyone was saying that he was too old for the job. So I rang Stan Bradshaw, one time tripe butcher in Padiham and a noted fell walker, and asked him about the notorious Tan Hill to Cat & Fiddle walk, a Rucksack speciality. This links the two highest pubs in Britain but unfortunately they are seperated by 120 miles of some of the toughest country you will find in this Sceptred Isle.

Stan said that he had done it when he was in his forties and found it very hard. "I did it again when I was 55 and it was much easier".

That is in the Rucksack tradition. Eustace Thomas was 53 years old when he ventured out on "A long circuit of the Fells for the amusement of the younger members of the Club". Twenty-one hours and 54 minutes later after ascending 25,500 feet of Lakeland hills he arrived back at his start point in Keswick, partook of a good meal and then climbed another 7 peaks to bring the total height gained to over 30,000 feet in 28 hours 35 minutes. Two days later he wrote that "I had not a single ache or any soreness to remind me of what Hirst calls one of my "notorious little do's"."

This book is full of "notorious little do's", the like of which no other club in the land can assemble. I am proud to be a member and would commend our first century to you.

Chris Brasher

Following page: Edale Head Rocks, Kinder
Photo by M. Cudahy

5

Chapter One
1902-1918
Foundation Stones

FOUNDATION STONES

The ancient Greeks had a saying; 'Not to know what was done in the world before we were born is always to remain a child'. October 13th 2002 marks the centenary of the Rucksack Club. The date is a challenge to the imagination, to think ourselves back to a world before we were born, to the rock from whence we were hewn. We are asked to go back to the Manchester of 1902, during the reign of King Edward VII and Queen Alexandra, to a group of cultured and courteous Edwardian gentlemen. They may have lived in a select, uppercrust mountaineering world very different from our own, but they built well, laying the foundations and traditions of a Club which guards its continuity.

The two founders or 'fathers' of the Rucksack Club were John H. Entwisle and Arthur E. Burns. Both founders claimed to be no more than 'novices – with a good walking record and a secret ambition to handle a rope and axe'. Clearly they were far from novices when they came to establishing a club.

There is some discussion between historians as to how Entwisle and Burns actually got involved in the Club's formation. What is beyond dispute is that in August 1902, both men responded by letter to a leader in the *Manchester City News*, 'In Praise of Walking Tours', extolling the virtue of being out and about on mountain and moor. It was a seminal letter. In it Entwisle and Burns complained that there was no Manchester based Rambling Club at the time. This fact is doubtful: in their book 'High Peak', an authoritative history of climbing and walking in the Peak District, Eric Byne (a Club member) and Geoffrey Sutton give the date of 1880 for the Manchester YMCA Rambling Club, though containing no mention of technical mountaineering adventures.

J. H. Entwisle

A. E. Burns

However, the public response to the letter was encouraging. Entwisle and Burns promptly struck while the iron was hot. A meeting was convened for Monday 13th October 1902, at the County Forum Hotel, Market Street, Manchester. The thirty men who attended unanimously agreed 'that a Club for climbers and walkers be formed'. The Rucksack Club was underway.

At the inaugural meeting on October 13th, 1902, Philip Minor was appointed treasurer - remaining in the post for 27years – and a levy of one shilling (5p) was collected. The newly formed club quickly got into its stride. Committee meetings and general business meetings proliferated during the first few months, and an inaugural dinner was held before the end of the year. An Outdoor Programme of Rambles was published from December 1903. The Club Library was commenced immediately. The Journal was established in 1907. The first Alpine Meet was held in 1909 and the Club's first hut was opened in 1912. Besides one-day and even afternoon rambles, climbing and caving took place at weekends and visits further afield when holidays permitted. During these first ten years a solid structure of ethos, values and traditions was laid. From the start, members regarded themselves as a 'fellowship'.

The advent of World War 1 in 1914 wrecked a chivalrous Edwardian Age, and along with it, deprived the Club of two fine senior members, but by then Club foundations were deep and strong enough to pull it through.

The rock from whence the Club was hewn provided a solid base for the next surge forward.

To the Editor of the Manchester City News

Sir, The general tone of the correspondence which has resulted from your leader on the pleasures of walking tours seems to indicate that this is an opportune moment in which to suggest the formation of a Ramblers Club for Manchester pedestrians. That such an institution would greatly enhance the pleasures of tramping and climbing we firmly believe. The pursuit of any hobby can be made to top the exhaustless sources of at least two forms of study, experiment and that which arises from the actual pure enjoyment, and that which arises from the actual which is derived from communion with kindred spirits. Man is everywhere a club-forming animal, and nowhere is it more evident than in this city of ours, where those whose tastes lead them to dip into the infinities of art, literature or science find close at hand communities of individuals whose tastes run in similar grooves to their own.

But strange to say that in the long lists of societies, no ramblers club has hitherto found a place. The nearest approach thereto is the Field Naturalists Society, but they – long life to them –spend their time "poking and peeping after things creeping" and offer no attraction to the young man who prefers to read Whymper on the Andes to Jones on the Blindworm. Now considering that in and around the city there reside at least half a dozen members of the Alpine Club – that Alma Mata of climbers and walkers – including an ex-president and vice-president, it is singular that here in Manchester, lovers of the moors and mountains have not ere this fraternized over their favourite pastime and sought around some common centre the delights of an interchange of experience. Yorkshiremen seem to be keener than ourselves, if we may judge by the number of signatures one sees in the visitors' books at inns in the remote dales of their own county, Snowdonia and the Lakes; and this keenness has found expression in the formation of the Yorkshire Ramblers' Club, a strong organization which has its headquarters in Leeds and publishes a journal of its doings annually. Its aims are briefly, but clearly defined in rule two, which reads; –"The objects of the Club are to organize walking and mountaineering excursions and to gather and promote knowledge concerning natural history, archaeology and folk-lore." Aprepos of the latter clause, one section of the Club devotes itself to the exploration of caves and from its researches comes practically our only knowledge of subterranean topography based on English authority. Every aspirant for membership is required to give proof of his interests in the objects of the Club, and to furnish a list of his climbing and walking expeditions.

Why should not Manchester possess such a Club? Dr. J. Collier of the Owens College, at the last annual dinner of the Yorkshire Ramblers, expressed his personal regret that there was no such institution in Lancashire, and certainly it would be surprising if in a population of three-quarters of a million there was not sufficient feeling to bring about such a result. The writers do not suggest the lines of operation. They are novices – with a good walking record and a secret ambition to handle a rope and axe. But if there are other enthusiasts of like passions who would welcome the idea here foreshadowed, they will be glad to cooperate.

J. H. Entwisle
A. E. Burns

29, Hulton Street, Moss Side
20.9.1902

A CLIMBING CLUB. FOR THE CITY AND DISTRICT

TO THE EDITOR OF THE MANCHESTER CITY NEWS

Sir, As a consequence of your publication on September 20 of our letter advocating the formation of a local club for walkers and climbers, several correspondents have expressed a desire to discuss the matter seriously. We have accordingly arranged to meet at the County Forum, Market Street, on Monday evening next, October 13, at eight o'clock and the invitation is extended to any of your readers who are sufficiently keen on the subject.

J. E. Entwisle
A. E. Burns

29, Hulton Street, Moss Side
11.10.1902

Societies
***

A CLIMBING CLUB.

THE MANCHESTER RUCKSACK.

The meeting convened through the columns of this paper for the thirteenth of last month drew together about thirty-five men, all keenly interested in the establishment of a club for local walkers and climbers. After a full and frank expression of opinion from a number of those present, it was resolved to form a club there and then, and a tentative committee was appointed to frame rules and consider suggestions as to the plan of action. Its resolutions were placed before a second general meeting held in the Deansgate Hotel yesternight week, and we cannot do better than quote from them in order to indicate the aims and objects of the Club and the lines upon which it is intended to be worked :-

The Club will be called The Manchester Rucksack Club.

Its object will be to facilitate walking tours and mountaineering expeditions, both in the British Isles and elsewhere, and particularly to initiate members into the science of rock-climbing and snowcraft.

A Club night will be held once a month, on the first Monday from 8pm until 10.30pm.

The primary idea of Club night will be to keep the members in touch with on another and with the objects of the Club, to read papers and to discuss relevant topics, and to give members a better opportunity of arranging expeditions.

This monthly meet of members will be a feature of the Club, it is anticipated, and will be found to be of the greatest possible mutual advantage. The joint secretaries appointed were Mr. A. E. Burns 88 Raby St., Moss Side, and Mr J. H. Entwisle 29 Hulton St, Moss Side. They will be glad to answer any inquiries or give further information. Intending members should make application before November 15. The enthusiasm displayed at the opening meetings, and the undoubted need for such an organisation in our midst, leads to the belief that under the leadership of local climbers and walkers of repute whom it is hoped to secure as presidents, the Club will earn for itself a place of distinction amongst the many societies of literary and scientific interest in the city.

THE FIRST PRESIDENTS

Harold Dixon

Joseph Collier

Charles Pilkington

The Club received immediate support from the leading mountaineers in Manchester, all of them eminent in mountaineering and their professions. The first President was Professor Harold B. Dixon of the Chemistry Department, Victoria University of Manchester. A leader in his field – with a C.B.E., F.R.S., two doctorates and also a member of the Alpine Club. He was celebrated for his climbs in the Canadian Rockies. The second President was Joseph Collier, F.R.C.S. He was a rock climber of strength - Collier's Climb, Collier's Chimney and more can be remembered. He was followed by Charles Pilkington, a former Alpine Club President, explorer of the Cuillin and the first to climb the Inaccessible Pinnacle.

The fourth President was Alfred Hopkinson who achieved the distinction of being knighted whilst being in office; not for services to the Club but for services to education. He was the first Vice-Chancellor of the Victoria University of Manchester. The active support of these Alpine Club men, and their friends, greatly helped to set the Club on the way.

By 1914 the Club had confidence enough to choose it's first "home-grown" President, Charles H. Pickstone, here shown carrying timber for the Club's new hut.
Photo by M. H. Adams 1913

13

THE FIRST MEETS

During 1902 and 1903 arrangements for walks and excursions were suggested at the monthly Indoor Meets, or arranged by the Committee from time to time. Rooke Corbett reported, in the 1914 Rucksack Club Journal "The first outdoor meet organised was on December 26th, 1902. The programme was a very modest one, a walk by paths and bye-roads from Millers Dale to Macclesfield, but cold air and a clear sky (not to mention the drinks stood by Minor at the Cat) contributed to a day of wholesome enjoyment".

The first Easter meet was held at Langdale in April 1903 but no detailed record of the event has survived.

LIST OF RAMBLES.

1903.

Dec. 13—Sun. Buxton, Axe Edge, Flash, Allgreave, Clulow Cross, Goostrees and Macclesfield.

" 26—Sat. Marsden, Wessenden Valley, Isle of Skye, Holmfirth and Penistone.

1904.

Jan. 10—Sun. Edale, Kinderscout, Downfall and Hayfield.

Feb. 14—Sun. Hope, Alport Dale, Bleaklow Hill and Woodhead.

Mar. 13—Sun. Glossop, Snake, Fairbrook Naze, Hayfield.

Apl. 1-4 EASTER MEET.

" 2—Sat. Penistone, Midhope Stones, Strines Moor, Moscar, Lady Bower and Bamford.

" 4—Mon. Chinley, Chinley Churn, Phoside Clough, Hayfield.

" 10—Sun. Hathersage, Eyam Moor, Baslow, Chatsworth, Ball's Cross, Bakewell.

" 23—Sat. Bakewell, Lathkill Dale, Monyash and Bakewell.

May 15—Sun. Greenfield to Crowden and Woodhead.

22-28 WHIT-WEEK.

" 28—Sat. Chatburn, Pendle Hill, Rimington.

June 12—Sun. Buxton, Earl Sterndale, Longnor, Hartington, Middleton, Youlgreave, Haddon and Bakewell.

1904.

June 25—Sat. Hope, Thornhill, Stanage Edge, Millstone Edge Nick and Grindleford.

Jly 9-10 SUMMER MEET.

" 23—Sat. Chatburn to Chatburn *via* Slaidburn and Harrop Fell.

Aug. 1—Mon. BANK HOLIDAY.

" 14—Sun. Bakewell, Ashford, Monsall and Miller's Dale, Buxton, Goyt's Valley and Whaley Bridge.

" 27—Sat. Frodsham, Hatchmere, Helsby Crag and Frodsham.

Sept. 11—Sun. Chinley, Rushup Edge, Mam Tor, Edale, Jacob's Ladder and Hayfield.

" 24—Sat. Mytholmroyd, Oxenhope Moor, Crimsworth and Hebden Bridge.

Oct. 16—Sun. Miller's Dale, Cressbrook Dale, Middleton Dale, Eyam, Eyam Moor and Hathersage.

Nov. 13—Sun. Delamere, Cotebrook, Eaton, Beeston Castle, Clotton, Wilsborrow, Delamere.

Members who are acquainted with any of the routes indicated, and are willing to act as leaders, are requested to communicate with the Rambles Sub-Committee.

The Weasel Pinnacle, Winster Rocks. *Photo by A. Briscoe*

From a report by G. T. Ewen:
"The first Summer Meet of the Club...was a great success. July 9-11 were days of brilliant sunshine. The Weasel Pinnacle was climbed by everyone, but...the amount of climbing and walking accomplished was certainly not remarkable, but that was more the fault of the sunshine than of the party...'It is too hot to climb!' was the general cry, and consequently much more was done in the way of striking graceful attitudes on the grassland at the foot of the rocks than in the way of climbing them".

Four members camped out, the main body occupied comfortable quarters at the Crown Hotel, at Winster.

Known present in camera, *left to righ*t:
Back row: J. Rooke Corbett, A. R. Horsfield, P. S. Minor, J. H. Entwisle
Front and middle: J. Uttley, G. T. Ewen

Remaining individuals, unknown position in photograph, but also present on the meet were: J. W. Whitworth, C. H. Ashley, J. Jackson, W. Milne, W. D. Moore, P. Ryan, H. Worthington.

Laddow Rocks

"Laddow Rocks may be described as the training ground of the Rucksack Club", according to the first guide to Laddow. Despite restrictions of access Laddow quickly became the Club's most used and favourite crag. Descriptions of the climbs at Laddow were printed in the Annual Report of 1904 and from time to time in following journals. Also, occasional articles were sent to and printed by the *Manchester Guardian*, as it was then known.

The photograph on the left was taken by Rooke Corbett and shows climbers on what was then called Right Twin Chimney, now known as Tower Face. The climbers have not been identified. A good stance and a firm hold of the rope appears to suffice for protection.

The Cave at Laddow Rocks, November 1903.

From the left the climbers are Anton Stoop, Arthur Horsfield, Arnold Bury, John Uttley, Philip Minor and Richard Broadbent. The photograph was taken by Uttley – he looks a little anxious as if he has just scuttled back in time after setting his camera. The Club was quick to explore Laddow Rocks. In those days landowners issued permits to climb on crags. Permission by a landowner was negotiated through the Club's 'Rights and Privileges Committee', and right up to the 1921 Handbook it was looked upon as 'a serious offence' should a member act contrary to an agreement.. Access to many crags placed the Club in a privileged position which it jealously guarded.. In 1908 Colonel Leigh granted permission for climbing on Laddow Rocks from the first Sunday in October till the Sunday before Whitweek of each year on advising the Keeper, Mr. Haigh of High Stones, Hadfield, of any intended visit.

THE CLUB AT LANGDALE, EASTER 1914

At all meets based on hotels group photographs were de rigueur in the early years. This meet was attended by 34 members and friends, the majority staying at the Old Dungeon Ghyll Hotel. The main party travelled by train to Windermere and were then driven to the O.D.G. This contrasted with two previous meets in Langdale when the parties walked in from Ambleside. One writer in 1914 seemed critical: "The first visit, 1903, in the dim and distant past (when all men were giants) was in the early and vigorous days of the Club. In those days men would walk miles to climb, would climb all day (and night too) and then thirst for more. In 1910 men scorned to ride in a conveyance...Has the Club reached the moribund stage?"

Committee men at the Old Dungeon Ghyll Hotel 1914.
From left to right: F. A. Dust, John Wilding, W. E. Bennison, P. S Minor, Herbert Baxter, C. H. Pickstone, H. E. Scott, A. E. Burns, W. E. Richards.

Steeple and Barlow in Skye, September 1911

On the Bealach a Mhaim.

View from the South Gorge, Ghreadaidh.

A corner of the camp.

In the Club Journal of 1911 Everard Wilfrid Steeple recounted a week spent camping on Skye with his great collaborator George (Guy) Barlow and two other friends. The weather was kind. Barlow's tent was about the same size as the Mummery, but heavier, having been built to withstand Skye gales. Of the other tent they used, "the owner informs us that it is possible to stand upright in it, if one stoops low enough". E. W. Steeple and Guy Barlow were great pioneers of Cuillin climbing from 1906 onwards, putting up at least thirty first ascents, including a great many new routes on Sron na Ciche and all the early routes in the Ghrunnda face of Sgurr Sgumain and Sgurr Alasdair.

The Glencoe Camp, 1904

The camp appears to have been a "first" for all the participants – Uttley, Entwisle, Wallwork, Stoop, Jackson and Kirk.

"Being adventurous spirits, nothing would suit us but Scotland", "A most doubtful choice from the point of view of the weather for our experiment". However, they reported that "We had been favoured with splendid weather…and our experiment of a camping holiday had been a conspicuous success".

J. Rooke Corbett emerging from Moonlight Gully, Ben Nevis, 1913.

J. Rooke Corbett

Many present-day members enjoy completing the "Munros" and the "Corbetts" and various lesser tick lists. The Club's leader in this particular field must be Rooke Corbett. In addition to inspecting and ascending all the mountains on his list, (of Scottish mountains of 2,500 feet and under 3,000 feet), Corbett was the fourth person to complete the Munros and the first Englishman to do so. He was an original Club member and the mainspring of the Rambles Sub-Committee. He was an honorary member and a Vice-President. He was a member of the first party to collect all "Welsh Threes" in one expedition, the others being Eustace Thomas and Wakefield in 1919. He was a Cambridge Wrangler, and as a student walked home to Manchester. He could play several games of chess simultaneously and could play a single opponent mentally while walking, if one could be found.

Brierley and Jeffcoat on Cader Idris.

A group of Club members at the entrance to Giants Hole, near Mam Tor, Derbyshire. Entwisle wrote in 1904: "The sport of swallet or pot hole hunting is a development of the last decade".

Philip Minor, Arolla, 1909.
Photo by Rooke Corbett

At the Bietschhorn Hut, 1913
From left to right: Adolf Muller, Kronig, Harry Scott, Charles Pickstone, Mrs C. H. Pickstone.
Photo by S. L. Pearce

Charles J. Pickstone with guide
Joseph Gentinetta above Zermatt.
Photo by S. L. Pearce

THE FIRST CLUB HUT

At the Inaugural Meeting of the Club Mr. P. S. Minor "thought it might be in the province of the Club to establish a Club house in the climbing area of the Lakes". This suggestion fell by the wayside, as did an approach by the Club to other climbing clubs of the time to consider a jointly owned hut.

In 1912, very largely due to the efforts of Stanley Jeffcoat, the Club opened the first climbing hut in Britain, Plas-yr-Ysfa in Cwm Eigiau, North Wales (pictured right). Initially this was a great success, but its use declined during World War 1. Thefts and vandalism forced the closure of the hut in 1920. During its use the rent was £3 pa., members fees were one shilling a night and guests paid one and six (5p and 7.5p).

"I wish another photo of the Club Hut could be given in the Journal; it's a certain cure for the shell-shock eyes, and the climbing light soon returns" – Note to the Editor from "somewhere in France". Club Journal 1914.

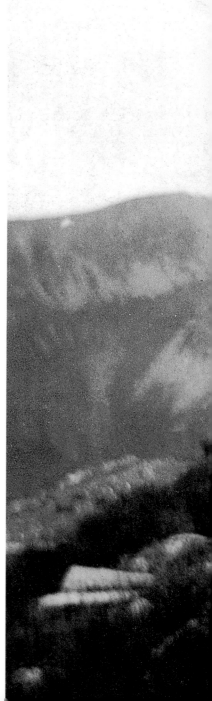

Plas-yr-Ysfa, Cwm Eigiau.
Photo by S. Jeffcoat

Meagre holidays and almost universal Saturday working confined most members to local hills much of the year, but affluent members could range more widely. These photographs were taken by the then S. L. Pearce, Manchester's Chief Electrical Engineer at the time. (This was before the National Grid, local authorities managed their own electricity supply). Pearce designed Barton and Battersea Power Stations, later becoming Sir Leonard.

The team comprised (lower photograph *left* to *right*): Charles H. Pickstone, President 1914-1916 and 1920. William Walker, Lord Mayor of Manchester 1932, knighted 1945, laid the foundation stone of the Haweswater Dam, 1935. Ernest Manning, former footballer and oarsman who went fox-hunting with the Lake District Fell Pack, who specially enjoyed "long days in remote hill country". Harry E. Scott, President 1921-1922 and 1943, a man who kept volumes of Rucksack reminiscences, from which these and other photographs have been obtained. And John Rooke Corbett, described by Philip Brockbank as "he of the great height and spade-like beard of well-nigh Assyrian magnificence", after whom the Scottish Corbetts are named.

Crossing the River Severn
Photo by S. L. Pearce

ANTON STOOP

In 1903 a Rucksack Club party to Laddow found a young stranger on one of the climbs, trying to puzzle out a route from a newspaper cutting. This was Anton Stoop, a Swiss who had been working in Manchester. As has so often happened, the chance meeting on a crag led to membership of the Club. Stoop was described as being brilliant on rock and a fine mountaineer in his native Alps. In October 1910 he lost his life on Nantlle-y-Garn. A group of large boulders collapsed as he climbed over them. The other two in the party had just climbed over the boulders quite safely. It was the Club's first mountaineering fatality. The news stunned and shocked Club members. The Annual Dinner was cancelled. "We have lost one of the bravest and kindliest of comrades. Few of us will forget the crushing weight of the announcement that he had lost his life on the Garn Mountain in North Wales", wrote his obituarist. Tony Stoop is buried in Llanllyfni Churchyard where the Club has a special memorial erected. This was found rather neglected and askew by Keith Treacher in 1990. Walter Riley then re-aligned the stone, and refurbished and refixed the two plaques.

J. Anton Stoop was a noted pioneer of Laddow Rocks where his first ascents of Leaf Crack and Cave Crack in old-fashioned boots anticipate modern developments. He came within the Club's orbit in a strange way. G. T. Ewen had published accounts of his exploration of Laddow Rocks in what was then the *Manchester Guardian* and out climbing one day Ewen was surprised to find a young climber half way up one of his routes with a copy of the newspaper in one hand. Stoop was Swiss by birth, an engineer working in north Britain. He was an able Alpine climber and an exceptional technician on rock.

Central Arête – Y Garn East Arête in background.

Anton Stoop's Memorial tablet at
Llanllyfni Churchyard

JEFFCOAT AND EWEN

Stanley Jeffcoat had been one of the prime movers in obtaining the Cwm Eigiau hut. He had spent much time and exerted prodigious effort to convert the property to a hut. His home crags were Castle Naze and Windgather where he had been the pioneer. His explorations of Scafell Pinnacle with Herford, Sansom and Laycock should have culminated in his being on the first ascent of Central Buttress, Scafell, but for once he was prevented from joining the party on that occasion.

George Ewen was an original member of the Club. It was his proposal to hold the first Alpine Meet in 1909. He had been elected a member of the Alpine Club aged about 32, with an Alpine record quite remarkable for a man of that age. It was his newspaper article that Tony Stoop was reading at Laddow.

2nd Lieut. S. F. Jeffcoat

Captain G. T. Ewen M.C.

Again, like Jeffcoat, Ewen was an innovator, the man behind the Club's first Alpine Meet in 1909. He also persuaded the Committee to agree to an annual Journal, bringing out the first edition in 1907 and the editing the first four issues. He moved from Manchester to London where he practiced as a Chancery barrister.

Stanley Jeffcoat was a tall, powerfully built, genial man. It was he who spearheaded the campaign within the Club to open a hut in Cwm Eigiau, in 1912, not only the Club's first hut but the first in Britain. Being a Buxton man, Windgather was close to hand, and as the 'discoverer' of Castle Naze, it was he who first introduced Siegfried Herford to the crag. He was a regular climbing companion of Herford's, linking closely with him in the early exploration of Scafell.

World War 1 had a devastating impact on the Club. Of 138 members at the time, 42 joined the armed forces, 7 of whom did not come through. Those who failed to return were Stanley Jeffcoat and George Ewen, Raymond Walter, A. D. Johnston, L. J. Oppenheimer, W. A. Hayes and C. S. Worthington.

Jeffcoat on the Scoop, Castle Naze. *Photo by Schaanning.*

Raymond Walter, killed in action on the Somme, July 14th, 1916.

When Raymond Walter enlisted in September, 1914, he left behind a sealed envelope, addressed to his father, to be opened after his death. The envelope contained the following letter:

Marple, Sept. 10th, 1914

Dear Father,

Death is a quest or a forgetting - in any case a fulfilment. When you open this note you will know that all is well with me.

I should like Uncle --- to have one of my books. Everything else I have is yours.
To ----, ----, and to my various friends who ask of me, a word of greeting.

And so goodbye.

Raymond.

Following page: Clogwyn d'ur Arddu
Photo by Ray Wood

Chapter Two

1918–1940

New Horizons

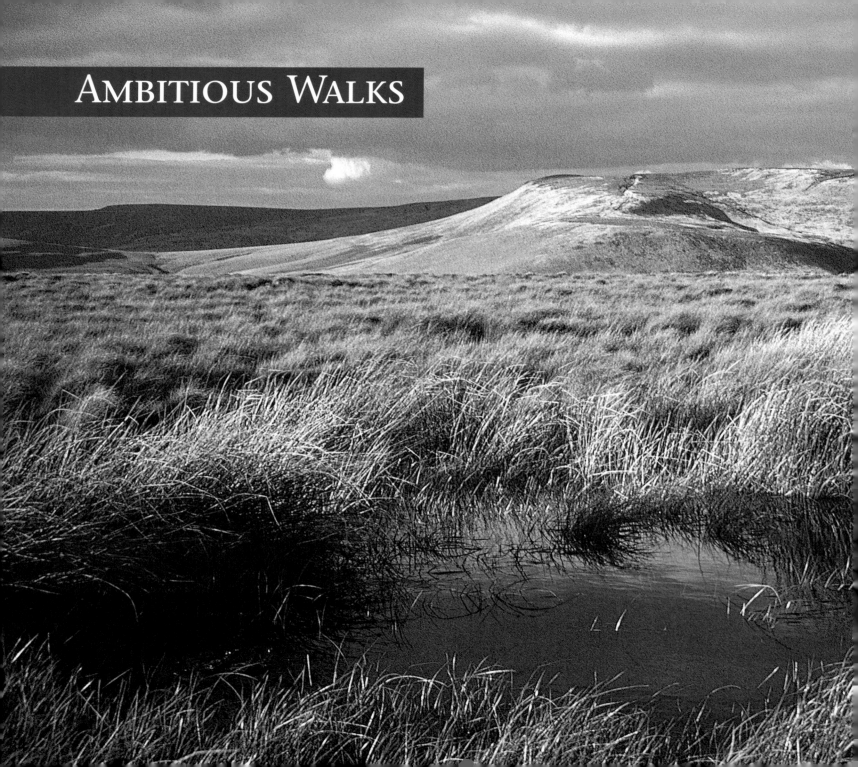

AMBITIOUS WALKS

Tough, ambitious hill walks have been the hall-mark of the Club from the beginning, and the years between the two World Wars proved no exception.

Close to home in the Peak District a number of walking achievements stand out. In 1919, with World War 1 barely finished, came the 37.5 mile Derwent Watershed originated by Eustace Thomas, Norman Begg, Alf Schaanning, William Walker and Bill Humphry. Then it was the turn of Fred Heardman, the Double Marsden Edale in 1923. Three years later Heardman was at it again, this time the 70 mile Colne Rowsley, in the company of John Firth Burton and Harold Gerrard.

No Club hill walker between the wars was more outstanding than Eustace Thomas, president 1924-25, an engineer by profession, who on a demanding outing seemed almost mechanically levitatated. He turned his attention to the Welsh mountains, the Lake District, the Scottish highlands and the Alps, where he became only the second man – and first Britisher – to scale all 4000m peaks. In 1919, in Wales, he linked up with Rooke Corbett and the Fell & Rock Climbing Club member A. W. Wakefield, for the first traverse of the Three-Thousanders. The Lakeland 'Fell Record' then beckoned. Thomas attacked the record three times (1919, 1920, 1922), the last successfully, 25,500 ft of ascent and descent, 66.5 miles, all within 24 hours. He was support party three years later when H. Gilliat and Fred Heardman traversed the Scottish 4000 ft summits, acting as chauffeur between Fort William and the Cairngorms.

Eustace Thomas at the Mont Fréti Hut.

Eustace Thomas in 1934 with his Avro Tutor. He soon traded this in for the improved performance of a Percival Vega Gull, which was requisitioned by the authorities at the start of WWII.

The Derwent Watershed near Outer Edge.
Photo by John Beatty

A Club Howff

Between the years 1927-1945 the Club leased Tal-y-Braich Uchaf in the Ogwen Valley.

As a focal point during a particularly active period in the Club's life it materially consolidated a sense of bonding or 'fellowship'. Aficionados looked upon the hut benignly as the ante-chamber to the gates of heaven and it gave birth to a whole generation of T-Y B'ers.

The hut acquired a wider mountaineering importance. Along with the Climbers' Club Helyg, opened in 1925, almost opposite on the A5 road, the hut acted as a springboard for the inter-war resurgence of Welsh rock-climbing. The hut's log book is a major source document for the period. All the significant first ascents are recorded; Pigott's Climb, Narrow Slab, Jubilee Climb, Main Wall Climb, Munich Climb, Grey Slab and a host of others. Every leading climber of the time has his name in the log. Within its pages can be found the first use of 'Cloggy' as an affectionate term and of Tremadog as a future crag to be explored. The log book is history in the making. The existence of climbers' huts is nowadays taken for granted. Tal-y-Braich Uchaf played a key part in resurrecting the hut idea and was in that sense ahead of its time. It has to be remembered that huts were still a novel idea in 1927 and that even by the start of World War 2 only five existed throughout the length of the country.

Tal-y-Braich Uchaf played its part in the establishment of both Capel Curig and Idwal Cottage Youth Hostels. Club member Jack Ashton, a leading light in the formation of the Youth Hostels Association in 1930, and the Association's first hostel warden, frequently used the hut on YHA business. In 1935, after some discussion, the Club affiliated to the new Association, a broadening of the social mix of those taking up mountaineering welcomed by J. H. Doughty in a Club Journal editorial.

During the period 1922-1936 a founder member, Charles Ashley had organised a series of annual dinners to keep the flame of Club 'fellowship' alight for those members domiciled in the south. These pleasant events proved to be the harbinger of the London Section, formally established at Gatti's restaurant in 1937, in the presence of Haskett-Smith. With its own outdoor programme and Winter lectures the Section continues 'to sustenance intelligent life South of Watford'.

In the same year Tal-y-Braich opened, the Club was actively involved in helping to start the Manchester University Mountaineering Club. From its link with the student life of the University and the YMCA the Club has recruited some of its finest members. Earlier, when Club member Wallace May moved to Birmingham, the Club supported his efforts to create the Midlands Association of Mountaineers. Content with his membership of the Rucksack Club, Wallace May had no wish to set up a separate club, only an 'association', but over the years the MAM has grown into an independent club in its own right.

Ice skating on Llyn Idwal, beneath the Devil's Kitchen cliffs, Ogwen.

Members and guests relaxing in the sun before a day in the mountains.

FIRST PARTY AT TAL-Y-BRAICH UCHAF, 1927

Between the years 1927-1944 the Club leased Tal-y-Braich Uchaf in the Ogwen Valley.

Names and faces recalled by Walter Riley, 1995.

From left to right: H. J. Taylorson, Eustace Thomas, R. W. James, Jack Ashton, Harry Summersgill, Harold Gerrard, John Wilding, J. Stanley Davies, Bill Humphry, Walter Riley, Herbert Baxter, Fred Heardman, John Uttley, Robert Burns, Bill Eversden.
Photo by Firth Burton

THE CLUB AT HOME

The exploratory impulse, the initiative to unearth fresh crags, and long distance walks, the ability to spot a line where others could not has been a characteristic of the Club from the beginning, and for which it soon became famous.

Pigott and friends climbing Crack and Corner at the Roaches Rocks. *Photo by Eric Byrom from Geoff Milburn Collection*

A. S. Pigott leading, and Morley Wood 'the perfect second', on the first ascent of Pigott's Climb on Cloggy, 1927. *Photo by J. Firth Burton*

The first Club member to try his hand on a new route was A. E. Barker, in 1906, on Yellowstone Gully, Cyrn Las. Cyrn Las as it turned out was a prophetic crag to do it on, the scene in 1935 of P. L. Roberts' and J. K. Cooke's superb Main Wall Climb. The value of a new route, apart from the adventure of tackling it in its own right, is that it is one way a Club member can make a contribution to the wider climbing fraternity. Main Wall Climb is there, and will remain there for future generations to enjoy. In that sense the Club's contribution over the years has been enormous.

During the period in question the Rucksack Club was home to a collection of rock-climbing giants, Manchester-based gritstoners, who turned their eyes to unclimbed rock in both the Lake District and Snowdonia. In the Lakes H. M. Kelly, President 1930-1931, presented a striking figure by climbing Moss Ghyll Grooves and the grit-like Tophet Wall as jewels in the crown. Over in Wales the wiry A. S. Pigott, President 1938-39, turned his attention to the sombre precipice of Clogwyn d'ur Arddu. In an inspired attack, after three previous reconnaissance expeditions, Pigott, ably supported by Morley Wood, 'the perfect second', and Lindley Henshaw and Firth Burton, put up the eponymous Pigott's Climb on the fierce-looking East Buttress, a psychological and technical breakthrough. Again in Wales, this time on Dinas Mot, in 1938, the tigerish Arthur Birtwistle accomplished Diagonal Route, a remarkable lead not repeated for 10 years, when John Lawton made the second ascent.

Whilst, naturally enough, Club members concentrated their efforts in Wales, Scotland was not neglected. The northern highlands, Ben Nevis itself, Glencoe and Ardgour and not least Skye, all received new routes.

Arthur Birtwistle making an early repeat ascent of Munich Climb on Tryfan in 1937. He is seen here using the toffee hammer from Tal-y-Braich to remove a pebble from a good thread belay point. *Photo by Ken Pearson*

The Munich Climb on Tryfan is so called to commemorate its first ascent by five Germans and John Jenkins during an exchange visit. During the ascent of Munich Climb the leader, Teufel, used three pitons. This was seized upon by some as an outrageous continental assault on British rock. The pitons were removed shortly afterwards by Menlove Edwards and party.

Harry Kelly climbing on Laddow Rocks.

Harry Kelly making the first ascent of Moss Ghyll Grooves on Scafell West Buttress, 1926.

Maurice Linnell moved from Stockport to Kendal as a boy. He attended Manchester University at the time when the climbing club was formed and soon teamed up with fellow Rucksack Club members, A. T. Hargreaves, Roy Horsman and Herbert Hartley to develop gritstone climbing, especially on Stanage.

However, his all too short career blossomed amongst the bigger hills. He led Narrow Slab on Cloggy and the girdle traverse on Pillar but the East Buttress of Scafell occupied his main interest with A. T. Hargreaves. In the 1934 journal he reported 5 new routes including Great Eastern and Overhanging Wall, but sadly the same issue carried his obituary.

Maurice Linnell.

At Easter 1934 he was finishing the ascent of the Castle on Ben Nevis with Colin Kirkus when a snow step collapsed and they were carried down a considerable distance, Kirkus though injured was able to secure the situation and go for help, but Maurice was killed instantly aged only 25.

Fred Pigott *left*, relaxing with friends.

ALFRED SEFTON PIGOTT, O.B.E. 1895-1979
'Fred' Pigott was an outstandingly fine climber. His new routes included Crypt Route on Bidean, Central Buttress on Coire Mhic Fhearchair and the famous routes on Clogwyn d'ur Arddu. He led the third ascent of CB on Scafell, then reckoned to be Britain's hardest climb. He was a committee member for many years, President in 1938-39 and was elected an Honorary Member in 1971. Fred was secretary of the Mountain Rescue Committee and its predecessors until he became chairman in 1955. He was later the first president of the M.R.C. For his services to mountain rescue he was awarded the OBE in 1964.

Pigott demonstrating belaying techniques that were employed on his early ascent of Scafell's Central Buttress.

Eric Byrom (seconding), traversing to the Oval on Central Buttress, Scafell, 1935. *Photo by C. D. Milner (Geoff Milburn Collection)*

...on Glyder Fawr
Photo by Eric Byrom
(Geoff Milburn Collection)

Harry Scott *left,* and Geoffrey Winthrop Young *right* high on Crib Goch. G.W.Y. was a frequent and popular attender of Club dinners shown in this rare photography with his artificial leg visible.

Menu frontispiece for the Club's 21st Anniversary Dinner held at the Albion Hotel.

THE RUCKSACK CLUB.

Coming-of-Age Dinner
SATURDAY, 10TH NOVEMBER.
1923

ALBION HOTEL,
MANCHESTER.

A difficult rescue took place in Derbyshire in 1928 involving Edgar H. Pryor, President 1926-27, who sustained a bad fall at Laddow Rocks, resulting in the loss of a leg. In 1932 A. S. Pigott and Morley Wood came across an injured and unconscious climber while walking over Crib Goch. After very arduous efforts they carried him down to Pen-y-Pass.

The problems encountered in getting these injured men down, led to the Club establishing a 'Stretcher Sub-Committee', which later joined forces with a similar body set up by the Fell and Rock Climbing Club. Out of this grew the National Mountain Rescue Committee under Wilson H. Hey, President 1936-37 as Chairman and A. S. Pigott Secretary.

It was one of the most single-minded contributions the Club made during the period to wider British mountaineering. The Mountain Rescue Committee in its turn evolved the 'Thomas Stretcher' designed by Eustace Thomas. The man who built the stretcher's proto-type was Walter Riley, an honorary member with 77 years of Club membership, now in his hundredth year and a living link between the Centenary and the inter-war years.

From 1935 onwards, Wilson Hey *left,* strived to persuade the Home Office to allow Mountain Rescue Posts to carry morphia, the final agreement was only reached in 1949 after Hey's fourteen year campaign, which included Hey creating and facing a precedential prosecution by supplying morphia in rescue kits.

Thomas Stretcher

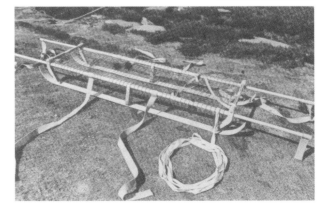

43

THE CLUB ABROAD

Founder member A. E. Burns *right*, and Gerrard on the Nadelhorn in 1926. *Photo by J. Firth Burton*

THE ALPS

During the inter-war years travel abroad tended to be restricted to an elite who had the cash and the time to undertake it. This affected what most ordinary members could do in the Alps or further afield. Yet Club members were surprisingly active.

The Alps were an obvious target. Chronologically, H. J. Mothersill was first in the field in 1903, successfully tackling the Funfingerspitze's Schmitt Kamin (before joining the Club in 1908), a route which even today presents its problems. Three years later R. B. Brierley, P. S. Minor and G. T. Ewen made an unguided traverse of Mont Blanc. From then on Club members were to be found in all regions of the Alps, the Oberland, Tarentaise, Dauphiné, Bavaria and the Pyrenees, climbing and walking. An undoubted achievement of note was Eustace Thomas completing his list of all the 4000m peaks. George S. Bower had the remarkable record of twenty-five consecutive seasons on the Chamonix Aiguilles. He knew the area better than many a local guide. His climbs included the first guideless repetition in 1923 of 'the great side of the Grépon', a fine technical achievement.

The summit of the Dent Blanche. *Photo by G. S. Bower*

Members gather to pose for photographs near the Mischabel Hut, 1926. Sitting far left is Harold Gerrard, sitting second from the right is Firth Burton. Wilson Hey on far right.

The imposing Lhonak Peak in Sikkim Himal, climbed by W. Eversden.

John Jenkins climbing the Mayer-Dibona route on the Dent du Requin, 1938.

Despite all the logistical problems, and the sheer dogged will to lift an expedition, Club members pushed into wild and remote parts. The springs of adventure stirred in the blood. The Sikkim Himalaya saw William (Bill) Eversden scale the imposing Lhonak Peak that so impressed Frank Smythe. John Jenkins and Michael S. Taylor set out 'Towards Ushba' in the Caucasus and returned with a collection of 'firsts'. Harry Spilsbury, President 1946-47, explored the ranges and glaciers of Norway, pioneering routes often by boat in the then remote Lofoten Islands, in the Horungtinder ascending the Skagastolstind, but above all, by the exposed south face, leading the first British ascent of Stetind in the Tysfjord region in the company of W. Priestley Phillips.

Harry Spilsbury *left*, Alan Deane and Arthur Burns, front. *Photo by Priestley Phillips*

The impressive Stetind 'The Anvil' 1381m lies above Tysfiord, Northern Norway *Photo by Priestley Phillips*.

Priestley Phillips and Harry Spilsbury on the summit of Stedtind.

Approaching the summit of Stedtind *a cheval*, along the narrow ridge. *Photo by Priestley Phillips*

Phillips seconding up the 'horizontal cleft that crossed the smooth and holdless wall'

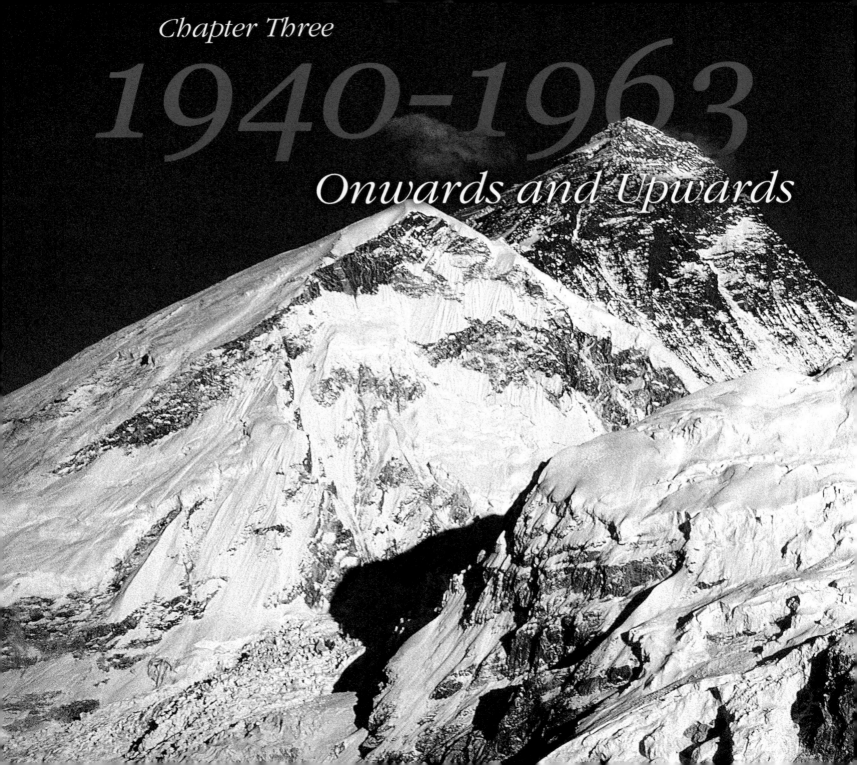

Chapter Three

1940-1963

Onwards and Upwards

THE WAR YEARS

The War Years curtailed Club activities severely. There were fewer meets and most were local to Manchester. Many younger members were away at the war. The Journal shrank and contained few contemporary articles. New climbs were made however, by Birtwistle, Lowe and Pearson. MUMC members accompanied by Rucksackers Cooper and Meade made the first circular walk out of the Welsh Three's from Pen-y-Gwryd. The frontispiece of the Journal for three years throughout the war was in colour to brighten the dark days, A rope stretcher was described by the Club after being carried by Gerrard and Stevens away from the scene of an accident. Cooper and Ferguson were members of the Home Guard of the Derbyshire Moors and patrolled on Bleaklow calling themselves the 94th Cavalry. A. E. Burns, an inaugural member and long serving secretary of the Club, resigned. Sadly among the wartime deaths recorded at this time were those of Steeple, Pryor, Chisman, and Speaker. Cooke was lost at Dunkirk, Burton in North Africa. Moffat met a tragically hard fate in the Far East, among many.

Peter Harding on the first ascent of Promontory Traverse, Cromford Black Rocks in 1945. Tony Moulam seconded the climb.
Photo from Peter Harding Collection

Vin Desmond and Arthur Birtwistle climbing the exit pitches of Red Wall on Lliwedd. *Photo by Alf Williamson*

Previous spread overleaf: Everest and Nuptse.
Photo by J. Beatty

In 1945-46 the number of meets and members attending increased enormously. The Club ventured further afield. Scotland was opened again to visitors after the Highlands were closed by the War Office. To visit Skye no longer required permission, this helped although petrol and food rationing continued and travel only eased slowly.

The Club was well represented on the newly formed BMC and Mountain Rescue committees. A complicated change of huts took place and occupied a large part of Club business. Activities on all fronts, in the Alps, rock and ice climbing, and walking all forged ahead with vigour, volume and standard.

Peter Harding on the first ascent of the Phoenix climb at Shining Clough, North Bleaklow.

Peter Harding making the first ascent of the gritstone classic climb Goliath's Groove at Stanage Edge in 1947. Harding was a pre-eminent post-war activist, also producing Robin Hood's Cave Innominate Superdirect Finish.
Photo by Ernest Phillips.
(Peter Harding Collection)

GOODBYE TO OGWEN

The years covered by the period 1940 to 1964 were in their way a consolidation of tradition, hard climbing on the crags and long treks across hill and moor. But first the difficulties and restrictions of World War 2 had to be faced and overcome. It was a sad day in 1945 when the tenancy of Tal y Braich was lost and the hut had to be given up (*above*). Whitsuntide Meet 1949. From l*eft to right;* Bill Roberts, Jack Clough, Lawrence Travis, Frank Colley, Arthur Bullough, Ken Pearson, Ron Battman. *Photo by C. D. Milner*

Entering Llanberis Pass at Beudy
Mawr. *Photo by John T. H. Allen*

Few documents reflect better the flavour of what it was like to be a climber when World War 2 closed in, than the old log book of the Club's Ogwen hut, Tal y Braich. The aspirations of young climbers called to battle, the frustrations, a sense of waste and loss are all to be found.

Petrol rationing meant that the hut was hard to reach, members doing their best by 'bike, train or thumb'. Windows of the building had to be blacked out in order to conform to defence regulations. Strange sounding military groups turned up for 'Toughening and Fieldcraft' courses. Food rationing led to a persistent cry from young men of an endless pit in the stomach. Yet despite all the problems members came, got out on the hills in defiant mood - and climbed. It says much for those active behind the scenes that the Club emerged from a dark period so strongly. But not without cost: Club members were lost at Dunkirk, in the desert of North Africa, the advance on Italy and in the air.

Following the closure of Tal y Braich, the Club's centre of gravity in the hills shifted from the Ogwen to the Llanberis Pass. Climbs and events in the Pass consolidated the Club's historic roots in the mountains of North Wales.

A last view into Tal y Braich.
Eddie Holliday prepares the
festive food.

THE OPENING OF BEUDY MAWR

The Club was dispossessed of Tal y Braich and adopted Tyn y Shanty, a little hut near the chapel on the A5. Great efforts were made to find somewhere more permanent and suitable. At this time the M.U.M.C. hut in Betws Garmon called Tyn y Weirglodd was used.

Bill Roberts made an enormous effort to find, secure and refurbish a hut in the Llanberis Pass for the Club. At last on April 24th 1947 his work was crowned with success as a lease was secured on Beudy Mawr at the foot of the Pass. Beudy Mawr opened for use in April 1948 with many members attending the opening ceremony by bus due to continued petrol rationing. To celebrate the opening, Peter Harding with Norman Horsfield climbed Trilon VS on Carreg Wastad, which today maintains a high standard in its grade. Soon afterwards a one-week long meet was held at Beudy accommodating 24 members!

Beudy Mawr 1949.

From left to right: Ted Moss, Alec Ferguson, John Hirst, Ken Barber, Eric Byrom, Ken Davidson, Ken Henshall gather in the doorway of the Gorphwysfa.

Members at the opening of Beudy Mawr.

The Climber's Grand Tour
Ken Davidson.

On a summer's day in 1947 Ken Davidson left Tyn y Shanty at 04.50 with the plan of a continuous walk connecting the major crags of North Wales and completing a solo climb on each. He climbed Great Gully on Craig-yr-Ysfa, Grooved Arête on Tryfan, Direct Route on Glyder Fach, up Tennis Shoe and down the Ordinary Route on Idwal slabs, Route II on Lliwedd and returned to the hut by 21.35. His only regret was that he had missed out on his planned ascent of Longland's – discretion being the better part of valour.

Ken Davidson, member 1946-95, was a serious photographer and often carried a large field camera into mountain situations, shown here enjoying a cigar with typical panache.

Ken Davidson creating a self portrait atop Glyder Fach, Ogwen. *Photo by Ken Davidson*

SHABBY TIGERS

Frequent visitors to Kinder Downfall area, *from left to right*; Vin Desmond, Alec Ferguson, Arthur Birtwistle, Vin Dillon, Joe Walmsley, Alf Williamson, unknown. *Back row from the left*; Geoff Pigott, Herbert Hartley, unknown.

TUNSTEAD

Tunstead - A Memoir by Vin Dillon

"For more than twenty years, in the 30's, 40's, and just into the 50's, Tunstead House, on the lower slopes of Kinder, was almost a second Club Hut for Rucksackers.

First run by Fred Heardman, then by Steve [Mac] Forrester after Fred left for Edale; then Kath Bryan joined Mac Forrester and Tunstead became the Rucksack home from home. Famous names knew Tunstead House; Winthrop Young, Frank Smythe, Eustace Thomas, among many. But whoever you were, once Kath and Mac had taken a liking to you, you became part of the Kitchen Tribe, part of the family, allowed to help with the washing up, debate music, books and crosswords with Kath, and try Mac's latest puzzles. The big kitchen table could seat twenty, and when the tribe included, and often did, Phil Brockbank, Jack Cooper, Fred Pigott, the Williamsons, Vin Desmond, Albert Dale, Taffy Davies --- the list could include half the Club ---- well, the famous hotpot went down by the bowlful, the stories ranged the world, and often enough, with Mac's encouragement and Kath's hands over her ears, we would sing the old songs, but always Mac's firm favourite, "Behind Those Swinging Doors" ....

A great time, and a great place......
Tunstead House!"

Kinder Downfall in Winter.

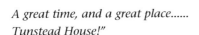

Fred and Milly Heardman took ownership of the Nag's Head in Edale.
Photo by Donald Berwick

Steve 'Mac' Forrester.

57

Trio Wall on Kinder Great Buttress in the Downfall Amphitheatre, was first climbed by Vin Dillon, Herbert Hartley and Vin Desmond. This area was extensively explored by Club members during the Tunstead House era.

Vin Desmond using a helping knee up from Herbert Hartley, who with Vin Dillon made the first ascent of the Girdle traverse of the Great Buttress, Kinder Scout.
Photo by V. T. Dillon

Vin Desmond takes up the popular local challenge of Pigott's Leap across the head of Crowden Brook.
Photo by V. T. Dillon

Vin Desmond waiting for the train at Chinley station.
Photo by V. T. Dillon

Desmond committed on 'Brockbank's stride' at Tunstead House. Phil Brockbank adjudicates!
Photo by V. T. Dillon

Founding member J. H. Entwisle made a remarkable walk from Land's End to John O'Groats at age 82. In fact Land's End to Manchester in time for the bowling season, then John O'Groats to Manchester, 1952.

JOHN ERIC BYROM

Eric Byrom joined the Club in 1936 and soon showed himself to be a first rate rock climber and alpinist. Pre-war, he climbed the hardest routes of the day; C. B, Pigott's, Belle Vue Bastion etc. and had many successful alpine seasons. His success in climbing was remarkable since his right arm was partially ineffective since birth. Eric was Club secretary for 30 years from 1942, made an Honorary Member in 1959 and President during 1974-5.

MILE UPON MILE

The Fiftieth Golden Jubilee Year of the Rucksack Club in 1952 was celebrated throughout the Club by a special annual dinner at the Engineers Club in Manchester and a Jubilee Meet in Langdale. The Manchester dinner was accompanied by an exhibition of mountain photographs.

During this celebratory year many new long distance walks were inaugurated. After some discussion with Fred Heardman, an audacious plan was made by Ted Courtenay to lead a party of Rucksackers to walk between the two highest public houses in England. A strong party of Ted Courtenay, Vin Desmond, Phillip Brockbank, Frank Williamson and Neil Mather left the Tan Hill Inn above Swaledale bound for the Cat and Fiddle near Macclesfield, 120 miles away to the south. After 54 hours Courtenay, Williamson and Desmond completed the longest Club walk so far attempted. (Brockbank and Mather who were forced to retire, successfully completed the walk the following year accompanied by Ted Dance).

The 1953 traverse. Nag's Head, Edale. *Left to right*, Dance, Brockbank, Williamson and Mather with Pickstone and Heardman who acted as transport officers.

The inaugural party departs from the Tan Hill Inn.1952. *Left to right,* Mather, Courtenay, Desmond, Williamson, Brockbank.

The 1952 inaugural party leaves Tan Hill at a pace.

Desmond, Jim Rostron and John Llewelyn on an early Garstang to Clitheroe.

Other excellent new walks were devised this year. Among the finest were the continuous traverse of the South Wales 2500s by Frank Williamson, Moffat to Peebles by Brockbank and Grassington to Langdale by Courtenay and Harvey. The first winter traverse of the Colne to Rowsley was made in 15 hours of darkness! An interesting long walk was completed following the mountain skyline of Snowdon by Vin Dillon and Ted Dance. Later that year, Dance also climbed Snowdon four times in one day by eight different paths. The Jubilee Meets list also included a Dane Marathon, Yorkshire 3 Peaks and Todmorden to Hayfield. It must be remembered that these walks were all completed as continuous walks unsupported, and with no sleep. The Club's reputation in distance walking was well established by the end of this vintage year heralding the way ahead for further innovation and record attempts.

ACTION IN THE ALPS

Immediately after the war there was a surge of activity in the Alps. The Club was on the move again despite a limited foreign currency allowance of £25. Ritson was active in the Bernese Oberland and Hirst and Milner climbed the Mittellegi Ridge on the Eiger. Members soon moved with other British climbers towards the harder new routes and came to equal the best of the continentals.

Geoff Pigott and Ken Pearson ascended the East face of the Caiman in 1949 with Andre Roch and Robert Gréloz. George Bower was very active in Chamonix also during this period. Byrom's newly formed alpine meets provided a springboard for members with Allan Allsopp on the Requin and Mer de Glace face of the Grépon in 1950.

During the meet, Pearson and Pigott maintained the principal lead whilst guests of Andre Roch *[left]* *Photo by Ken Pearson.*

From left to right: Fred Pigott, Andre Roch, Ken Pearson. *Photo by Ken Pearson*

East Ridges of the Aiguilles du Plan and Crocodile, Chamonix. *Photo by John Hartley*

Neil Mather climbed the Schalligrat in '51, and with Albert Ashworth, the Peuterey Ridge in '52, Pigott with Ashworth made major ascents of the Ryan Lochmatter on the Plan, the Frontier Ridge of Mont Maudit and the Aiguilles du Diables. Dick Meyer and Gordon Dyke were successful on the North face of the Cima Grande and the Yellow Edge of Piccola. Dance and Moseley climbed the Couturier Couloir on the Verte. A large group of members gathered in Zermatt and climbed the Dent d'Herens by the north-northwest face after several attempts. The team included Dillon and Courtenay. Dennis Davis was active too, climbing the Route Major on the Brenva Face of Mont Blanc, and with Ray Colledge he added the north faces of the Triolet, the Plan and the Bionnassay.

Gordon Dyke climbing the North Face of Cima Grande. *Photo by Bill Bowker*

Alec Ferguson on Adang Kamin in the Italian Dolomites.
Photo by Ken Davidson

Left to right: Dance, Courtenay, Jessie Byrom, Dillon, Desmond, and Eric Byrom.

Crossing the Tieffmatenjoch on the Dent d'Herens. Climbers are 'bassist' Ron Smith and Fred 'the farmer' Boardman. *Photo by V. T. Dillon*

'Last man down'. The final descent through the icefall from the North-west face of the Dent d'Herens. *Photo by V. T. Dillon*

Albert Ashworth seconding Rock and Ice member Don Willans on the first ascent of Forked Lightning Crack at Heptonstall Quarry, Lancashire. NB: The runner visible, a wooden wedge, was the only protection on the climb. Woolworth's black plimsoles were worn by both climbers.

Photo by John Hartley

The North Manchester Brigade became reinforced by John Hartley, Bill Bowker, Edwin Legget and Roger Whewell. Richard Harris and Maurice James joined them also and amongst the many great climbs done were: north face of Piz Badile in 1961, north face of the Dru in 1962 and south face of Punta Gugliemina. This team climaxed in 1964 with ascents by Bowker on Southwest Pillar of the Dru, Harris on the east face of the Capuchin, whilst Hartley made a complete traverse of the Chamonix Aiguilles in just 4 days.

Back in Britain during this period, rock climbing was achieving ever higher standards. This was a tremendously active and successful period for the Club, and inspirational for future members.

Dave Briggs, a leading post-war alpinist.
Photo by Ken Davidson

1955 Merseyside Himalayan Expedition at Liverpool Docks awaiting embarkation to India. *Left to right*; Peter Boultbee, Ted Courtenay, Dennis Davis, Charles Booth, Alfred Gregory.

These expeditions, demanding dogged will and courage, were a consolidation of a tradition set by member Reginald James on Shackleton's legendary Endurance expediton. In terms of organization, mode of travel, and sheer time away (six months in one instance), they marked the end of an era. A new sort of expedition was about to take over.

Rowaling and Beyond

In 1955 Alfred Gregory, fresh from his experiences high on Everest in '53, joined an expedition to the remote Rowaling Himal. Ted Courtenay was invited along with members of the Wayfarers Club and led by Dennis Davis. They explored the Menlungtse area and made first ascents of 19 peaks between 19,000-22,000 feet.

Davis went on to join Charles Evans to attempt Annapurna II, but although they were turned back from this summit by the conditions, they made the second ascent of Annapurna IV.

In the same year, Gregory went on to lead a party including Dave Briggs and Dennis Davis to attempt the ascent of Disteghil Sar. A route was established to Camp 4 at 21,500 feet in poor weather but the attempt was abandoned after prolonged snowfall made conditions impossible in the time available.

Also in '55 Rucksack Club member Neil Mather was invited to join an expedition to attempt the first ascent of Kanchenjunga. The party also included Joe Brown, George Band, Charles Evans, John Jackson, Tom McKinnon and John Clegg doctor. After helping to build the supply chain up the mountain Mather helped to set up camp 6 from which a successful summit bid was made by Brown and Band the next day.

The turn of the decade saw Geoff Smith with Noyce's party on the first ascent of Trivor in the Karakoram, Handley, with a Derbyshire expedition to Kulu, whilst Harold Mellor climbed 21,700 foot Bara Shigri.

Dennis Davis.

Rowaling Himal 1955. Descending from Ramdung Peak. Gauri Shankar in the background. *Photo by Dennis Davis*

MASHERBRUM

The first major expedition to a big peak organised by the Club was to Masherbrum (K1) in the Karakoram in 1957. Walmsley (who led), Dance and Geoff Smith of the Club, together with Bob Downes, Don Whillans and Dick Sykes employed six Balti high altitude porters.

Base camp was set up at 13,000 feet on the Masherbrum glacier after an approach march from Skardu by the Indus, Shyok and Husk valleys.

A route was prospected to Camp 7 at 24,800 feet on the South-East face, spearheaded by Whillans and Smith who attempted the summit but were defeated by poor snow. Dance and Sykes, coming up to take over, had to join them and all were confined by bad weather for three days in a two-man tent, during which time Dance was incapacitated by an altitude related condition. He recovered when they were able to descend. Walmsley and Downes, who had spent ten days in the valley, having also recovered from chest trouble, took over the lead.

Walmsley, Downes and a porter returned to Camp 6 where they were pinned for six days by bad weather. Unfortunately, Bob Downes's pulmonary oedema returned with fatal results. The team returned up the mountain to collect Bob's body which was carried to Skardu and buried there in a lovely situation.

During the expedition high altitude sickness struck most members of the team. Tragically Bob Downes died during bad weather in a high camp. *Photo by E. W. Dance*

25,660 FT.

— HIGHEST POINT REACHED

S.E. FACE.

VII

VI

FANNY

SERAC PEAK

V

IV

III

DOME

ICE CLIFFS

ICE CLIFFS

SERAC BASIN

II

I

SERAC GLACIER

SCALY ALLEY

Diagramatic picture of
Masherbrum drawn
by Bob Downes.

Camp 4 on
Masherbrum
with Chogalisa
in the distance.
Photo by E. W. Dance.

Walmsley and Whillans then made another summit attempt, but were again defeated by the snow conditions. They took to the rock but only managed two very severe pitches in that day and retreated 300 feet from the summit. Time and supplies were running out and they descended.

NUPTSE

The next major expedition during the early 1960's was to 26,000ft Nuptse. Joe Walmsley the leader, Dennis Davis, Jimmy Lovelock and the rest of the team travelled by road in two Vanguards to Nepal. The chosen route, up the middle of the south face posed difficult sections. Eight camps were established from which a successful summit bid was made by Davis and Tashi sherpa on May 16th 1961. The following day Chris Bonington, Les Brown and Jim Swallow also succeeded in reaching the summit.

Tashi Sherpa on the summit of Nuptse in 1961.
Photo by Dennis Davis

Nuptse 7,879 metres. *Photo by Dennis Davis*

Nuptse 1961. Chris Bonington at the foot of the 'V' chimney on the ridge to Camp 3. *Photo by Dennis Davis*

Nuptse 1961. Joe Walmsley climbing below Camp 3. *Photo by Dennis Davis*

Nuptse 1961. Tashi sherpa on fixed ropes level with Camp 3. *Photo by Dennis Davis*

Chapter Four

1963–1980

The Big Days

Bivouac on the Walker Spur.
Photo by "Bivouac" Bill Bowker

CLIMBING BECOMES MODERN

The Club's tradition of long and tough outings and outstanding achievements was well upheld during the period covered by 1965-1980. But in essence the period was a transitional one. Tradition was extended to embrace a dawning climbing world of new possibilities.

Two developments had come on the scene. A radical functionalism took hold in the design and production of clothing and equipment added to by a revolution in road and air travel. The two factors combined changed attitudes and expectations. What seemed impossible in 1965 had become normal fifteen years later.

The change becomes evident in both the formal and informal activities of Club members.

The better designed and tested equipment led to a plethora of safety 'protection'. In 1965 it was still possible to see the occasional bowline tied around the waist. By 1980 the bowline had been replaced by the harness and the old-fashioned beret by the helmet.

White Slab HVS,
Clogwyn dur Arddu.
Photo by John Hartley

Shrike HVS a spectacular steep wall climb overhanging
the higher reaches of the East buttress of Cloggy.
Photo by John Hartley

There is a sense of course, in which Siegfried Herford's bold 1914 lead of Scafell's Central Buttress can be said to have inaugurated the modern era of rock-climbing. Club members such as H. M. Kelly, A. S. Pigott and P. R. J. Harding inspired an extension of the psychological and technical boundaries. But it took the advent of the new equipment during the period under review for modernity to really get a grip amongst the rank-and-file of members.

Once the full possibilities had been grasped, things began to change swiftly, with a new type of young climber doing harder routes coming into membership. Classic, traditional homeland routes continued to receive attention. Cloggy was revisited with new vigour. But the repertoire took a leap forward, with Club parties to be seen tackling the isolated sea-stacks of the Old Man of Hoy and the Old Man of Stoer.

Mangoletsi HVS, on Pant Ifan, Tremadog. This photograph first appeared on the cover of Issue no.1 of *Mountain*. *Photo by John Hartley*

Dawn after the second bivouac. John Beatty descends the ridge towards Sgurr Fhearthaich. *Photo by R. Beighton*

The Cuillin of Skye in winter conditions. John Beatty with Rob Beighton traversed the entire ridge during a cold settled spell in February 1978. Three bivouacs were required and fourteen abseils were made over three days. Climbing one day behind were John Allen with Mike Edwards, who were less lucky with the conditions, which deteriorated, causing them to abandon their attempt at Sgurr na Banachdich.
Photo by R Beighton

During the abseil descent of Am Bhasteir, the ropes jammed behind an ice bollard. Here, Rob Beighton is tugging hard, hoping a loose end will run free. *Photo by J Beatty*

In the dry summer of 1976, Barry Thomas *(above)* and John Beatty climbed The Old Man of Hoy and many other mountain crag classics. *Photo by J. Beatty*

John Allen only just returning from a successful ascent of the Old Man of Stoer. *Photo by J.Beatty*

Old Man of Stoer near Lochinver. *Photo by J. T. H. Allen*

The Old Man of Hoy, Orkney. *Photo by J. Beatty*

77

Bill Bowker climbed Walker Spur on the Grand Jorrasses in 1967.
Photo by Bill Bowker.

Eddie Birch dressed in the period costume of Hadow during television re-enactment sequences on the Matterhorn.

Eddie Birch on a winter ascent of the Matterhorn North Face - with Eric Jones, Leo Dickinson, Brian Molyneux, and T.V. cameras
Photo by Leo Dickinson (Eddie Birch Collection).

Rob Beighton preparing an abseil from the summit of Pointe Wellzenbach, one of the four towers on the South Ridge of the Aiguilles Noire de Peuterey, 1979.
Photo by J. Beatty

The tragic fatality of Richard Harris occurred in 1966 on the Sentinel Rouge, Brenva Face of Mont Blanc, depriving the Club of its recently appointed Journal editor.
Photo by John T. H. Allen.

Lyn Noble descending the Coeurgrat on the Obergabelhorn after climbing the north face route with Dave Pownall.1979
Photo by D. Pownall

High Moss

Ever since Minor broached the question of a Lakeland hut at the Inaugural Meeting of 1902, the Rucksack Club had shelved all such proposals in favour of developments in Wales.

The subject was raised again with urgency by Tom Waghorn at a committee meeting in 1963. Byrom recorded in his minutes, "several members supported a motion by T. Waghorn that the Club should acquire a hut in the Lake District......"A cursory investigation in Eskdale was made. Further efforts were made the following year when the Committee began to consider the urgency after appeals in the A.G.M. of 1964. Brian Rhodes was instructed to investigate options in the Lakes. A dilapidated barn was discovered at High Moss House on the Turner Hall Farm in the Duddon Valley. Much discussion took place to consider that it might be too remote, unpopular and expensive. The owner wanted £600, agreement was finally reached, and sub committees were formed to develop the rebuild project. Many members became involved in both legal and structural discussions over the next two years.

After four years of negotiation between stalwart undeterred members and the architects, quantity surveyors, builders and the Treasurer, the Club had confidence to elect a hut warden. Brian Richards accepted the job and set about assembling working parties and decorating and furniture building ready for the opening.

At last, on Saturday May 18th 1968 the President Frank Kiernan performed an opening ceremony before a multitude of guests and members. It had been sixty-five years, seven months and four days after Philip Minor had first expressed his thought for a hut.

The opening ceremony of High Moss took place on May 18th 1968.

Frank Kiernan was a Club member for 74 years, a prodigious walker who was regarded as the dominating personality of the Marsden-Edale in the thirties. His claims to ill-health belied his ability to cover the ground at a rate causing despair amongst his colleagues. The meets he led in Langdale until his eightieth birthday were legendary, attracting large numbers from all sections of the Club. In his retirement he gave unfailing encouragement to younger members and their ambitions, and would frequently appear in support of long distance walks. On one memorable occasion this turned out to be afternoon tea on his lawn in Bowness.
Photo by F. Solari

Ian Grant, *left*, and Fred Pigott *right*, in discussion on the opening day of High Moss.

High Moss part way through the rebuild stage in 1967.

High Moss at time of purchase, 1964.

BIG WALKS

An appetite for extended long walks developed to fever pitch within the Club. Not only were novel routes conceived, mostly joining places with club associations, but speed became the touchstone. A new group of fast men were emerging, charged with historical reference and commitment to innovate.

During a long weekend in 1965, Dennis Davis with a party of Karabiner Club members enjoyed a Snowdon to Brecon Beacons walk extending south across the high ground of the Berwyn and Plynlimon.
The Club organised its first orienteering event (a new navigation sport recently popularised from Scandinavia) and chose Macclesfield Forest as a suitable venue. Ted Dance and Bob Astles became accomplished and competed for England in various international events.

Ted Dance and Bob Astles in Eskdale.

The first two-day Mountain Marathon was set around Muker in Swaledale. Members taking part were Richardson, Talbot, Astles, Mather and Dance.
Photo by E. W. Dance

82

Geoff Bell on The Schill in the Borders at the end of a fast unsupported Pennine Way. *Photo by Mike Cudahy*

By 1967, the challenge of short winter daylight enticed Stan Bradshaw, Dennis Weir and John Richardson to attempt the already classic Tan Hill to Cat and Fiddle route to be attempted in deepest winter. The conditions were utterly miserable for the entire duration of the walk but success was achieved in a time of 51 hours and 49 minutes.

The high tops of Scotland had always fascinated the Club since the first traverse of the Scottish Four's of Eustace Thomas and Begg, over five consecutive days. In 1954, Brockbank and Williamson attempted the first traverse to be done entirely on foot. Beyond the Cairngorms, Brockbank retired with Williamson continuing alone to complete the route. A year later, Desmond with Jim Rostron completed a second traverse, eventually hitch-hiking home by way of a fish lorry, a police car and a taxi.

Brian Cosby and Arthur Clarke opened their scorecard in 1967 with a 48 hour traverse. Following this, Stan Bradshaw and John Eastwood completed the traverse, and again in 1974 with Don Talbot and Neil Mather.

In the same year came an epic repeat of Eustace Thomas's Lakes 2500s, 77 summits, 105 miles and 13,126m of ascent. In a tour de force, Stan Bradshaw, Ted Dance and John Eastwood completed the round in 72 hours.
A new two day Mountain Marathon 'event' had been organised, the Rucksack Club appeared on the startline. John Richardson and Don Talbot, Neil Mather with Jack Bloor of the Gritstone Club and Ted Dance and Bob Astles were first home. The event became annual and in 1972 Karrimor began its famous sponsorship. Every year since then, the Rucksack Club has been honoured with high finishing places in the elite category with Richardson and Cudahy completing 21 years in the elite race. Fell running had become an accepted part of the mountain scene.

An Anniversary Walk from the High Moss hut to Edale was in the 75th Jubilee Year of 1977. Eight started and five finished plus a dog. Dance, Bell, Cudahy, Courtenay, Mills, Richardson, Talbot, and Grant took part.

The Scottish Fours were repeated in 1977 by Richardson, Cudahy, Grant and Mackenzie (guest), the first two in a very fast time of less than 38 hours.

Between 1972 and 1978 Rucksack teams were first in the High Peak Marathon with teams formed variously from Dennis Weir, Ted Dance, John Richardson, Mike Cudahy, Geoff Bell and Don Talbot.

In 1978 Geoff Bell completed a solo-self-sufficient Pennine Way in 5 days 16 hours 14 minutes, and recorded that "it is much more pleasant to go a little slower, to call at hostelries and to have good companions".

A 1979 a winter Tan Hill to Cat and Fiddle was completed by Bell, Richardson and Cudahy with Dance leaving the party early in Lancashire. Also in the same year, Bell and Cudahy completed an audacious 140 mile North Wales Horseshoe, the Club's longest continuous walk.

The Rucksack Club tradition of hard long distant walks was pre-eminent, yet there were members in the wings, ready to challenge and innovate.

The 75th Jubilee Anniversary Walk from High Moss to Edale. This 114 mile walk was conceived by Geoff Bell, one of the five finishers from a party of eight. 1977. *From left to right,* Taffy Davies, Mike Cudahy, Dennis Weir, Ian Grant, Geoff Bell, Ian Courtenay, Ted Dance Ted Courtenay, John Mills, Don Talbot and Graham Poole. *Photo by Geoff Bell.*

John Eastwood *left,* and Arthur Clarke *right*, at the end af a successful traverse of the Scottish Four's, 1967. *Photo by Brian Cosby.*

HIGH CAMPS

Early High Camp on Y Garn. *Photo by V. T. Dillon*

High Camp memories after being asked to 'sub'....

Lead a high camp on Tryfan? Followed remit of 'camp on top'. The tents perched on flatish boulders next to Adam and Eve. Visiting late arrivals lodged in the gullies below the twin stones. Watched Tryfan's sunset shadow sweep into darkness. Wine at nine in the meet leader's quarters. Whisky had replaced the wine long before I can remember. It was found to have a greater payload coefficient. Food techniques: Does the high camper travel with total self sufficiency portering up three course meals and the silver, or tank up at the chippy in the valley and hope the night isn't too long. The number of people physically capable of getting into a tent is extraordinary, though it does decline through the evening. The manufacturers do give recommendations on the number of occupants. This is from observation, clearly an understatement, perhaps in order to increase tent sales.

David Dillon

Summit rocks of Tryfan. *Photo by V. T. Dillon*

"It began in the late 50's, after a night crossing of Kinder, with Vin Desmond. We thought "the high places, remote and lonely, beauty and silence, the high table of the gods"... So we tried it. Glyder Fach, 1959. Just the two of us. Right on top. Rainstorm, no flysheet, bags awash... We fell for the feel of height and isolation. Then sadly Vin Desmond died, but we'd begun.

Thus the Rucksack High Camps became part of the outdoor programme for thirty years, every September. The "remote and lonely" bit was the first to change as the tents multiplied. The idea of ferrying big loads up to high summits for a night of beauty and silence inexplicably took hold.

In '68 on Pen yr oleu Wen - 17 remoteness seekers in 10 tents and all 17 were accommodated for 'wine at nine' in the leaders 4- man tent. In '75, on Elidyr Fawr, a rose tinted dawn rose on 9 tents, 16 campers. In '86 Cader Idris - 30+ including 4 ladies. All the Welsh 3's were done except Crib Goch and Snowdon, both for obvious reasons. All the Lakes 3's were done and one Scottish 3, - Schiehallion. Then we began to revisit old favourites again - and again. The great moments were sunsets, dawns, storms, wine at nine in the leader's tent, stories, singing and the starlit stagger back to the tents. Solitude and beauty remained: we loved it all. Every High Camper will have his or her own own special memories. Mine - standing with this friend or that, looking up at the great star constellations at midnight, blazing in skies untroubled by civilization. That and 17 guys and dolls in a 4 man tent, quaffing, storytelling, pole bending.

After the 31st camp in 1990, the baton of silence and beauty was handed to Carole, an experienced High Camper who will carry the series with grace until 2020."

Vin Dillon

The igloo building series of meets began in 1970 inspired by Rob Beighton and continued by Gordon Adshead for thirty years. All the Scottish Fours and many of the high Munroes were visited. Stories of epic nights and lost summits are legion. *Photo by J. Beatty*

Peter Shortt emerging from a long night on the ice. Ben Nevis. *Photo by J. Beatty*

Ted Courtenay at Loch Coire an Lochain, Braeriach. *Photo by J. Beatty*

THE WORLD OPENS OUT

A major change was the way remote regions and higher ranges which in 1965 still seemed the preserve of a monied class had, by 1980, become a 'playground' for groups of Club members who climbed together as friends. In previous generations individual Club members had taken part in various expeditions, but this was a new phenomenon. The number and composition of the parties had changed.

A cluster of small but well-organised parties left home shores to take on fierce adversaries with Roger Whewell in the Atlas, Arthur Clarke in East Greenland, Brian Cosby in Hindu-Kush, John Allen on Malubiting, Nampa and Phabrang in Nepal, Eddie Birch on the South Ridge of Fitzroy, and Tim Leach on the West Ridge of Guari Sankar. These were all tackled with dogged determination and a fresh technical mastery. The world had become the climber's oyster.

In 1966 a Manchester Hindu-Kush Expedition was formed by Cliff Meredith as leader, with Ian Bell, Pete Booth, Brian Cosby, Steve Crowther and Bill Rowntree who climbed and surveyed in the area around Koh i Bandaki in northern Afghanistan.

By 1968 John Allen had formed a Manchester Karakoram Expedition to Malubiting 7,453mtrs, with Ian Bell, Arthur Clarke, Brian Cosby, Ian Grant, Tom Waghorn, and Oliver Woolcock and Brian Ripley joining from the Karabiner Club. Sadly, Brian Ripley died in a fall from the highest point reached.

Nampa, western Nepal 6755m.
Photo by J. T. H. Allen

Camp 3 on Nampa, western Nepal, i970.
Photo by J. T. H. Allen.

Arthur Clarke made an exploratory expedition led by Derek Fordham to east Greenland for mountaineering, exploration and sledge-hauling in 1969.

A Karakoram Expedition in 1970, with Eddie Thurrell, Cliff Meredith, Trevor Braham and Mike Briggs, climbed minor peaks in the Daintar Valley above Gilgit. Exploration of the area was mostly made with an RAC road map. In December 1972, Eddie Birch made the first ascent of the south ridge of Fitzroy in Patagonia. All six members of the Expedition reached the summit.

1974 John Allen, Brian Cosby, Ted Courtenay, Cliff Meredith, John Beatty and Jeff Mason avoid the crowded Alps and holidayed in the Himalaya. Allen, Mason and Cosby climbed Phabrang 6172m.

Rob Beighton making chapatis on the approach to Nampa in western Nepal.

John Allen returned to Western Nepal in 1970 to climb Nampa 6755m a remote peak identified by W. H. Murray. Rob Beighton, Yvonne and Arthur Clarke, Brian Cosby and Bill Rowntree travelled overland by lorry during a four month expedition. Cosby and Beighton climbed to within 300m of the summit.

1979 saw Tim Leach on the Guari Sankar West Ridge Expedition, reaching within one metre of the South Summit. "An exciting adventure on a formidable and beautiful mountain"

Arthur Clarke explored the remote east coast of Greenland in 1969. *Photo by Arthur Clarke.*

Fitzroy in Patagonia. All six members of the expedition reached the summit.
Photo by Eddie Birch

Eddie Birch on the summit of Fitzroy in 1972.

Cliff Meredith and Steve Crowther surveying and mapmaking for the R.G.S. in a remote region of Koh i Bandaki in the Hindu Kush 1966. *Photo by B. Cosby*

Brian Cosby, *front,* and Steve Crowther on horseback in the Hindu Kush, "after a scuffle with villagers", 1966. *Photo by B. Cosby*

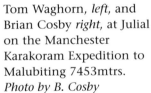

Tom Waghorn, *left*, and Brian Cosby *right*, at Julial on the Manchester Karakoram Expedition to Malubiting 7453mtrs. *Photo by B. Cosby*

From left to right, John Allen, Jeff Mason and Vinod Gugliani on the summit of Phabrang 6172m on the Indo-Kashmir border. 1974. *Photo by B. Cosby.*

Chapter Five

1980-2002

Forever Young

Yosemite, El Capitan headwall.
Photo by Ryan/Deakin

LOOKING TO THE FUTURE

As the Rucksack Club celebrates its 100th anniversary in 2002 it can look forward to the next century with optimism and enthusiasm. A review of the period 1986 to 2002 shows that the Club is as strong and active as ever.

As travel opportunities and leisure time have increased so have the Club's activities. All around the world Rucksack Club members have made their mark. This has included major ascents of 'big walls' in America, 1st ascents in the Greater Ranges and the Arctic, caving exploration in Europe and notable ascents in the Alps.

It is at home however where the ongoing strength of the Club lies maintaining the tradition of long distance walking and climbing at all levels. The outdoor meets programme is central to the Club's success and it has continued to flourish and to reflect the varied activities and essence of the Club with members being able to enjoy long walks, fell running, cycling, climbing and mountaineering meets. At a time when some other clubs are finding it difficult to attract new members the Rucksack Club goes from strength to strength with an increasing membership.

In this period important changes have taken place within the Club. In 1990 the rules were amended to enable women to gain membership and to play a full and active part in the life of the Club. In 1993 Craigallan, the Club's Scottish hut, was acquired giving members excellent bases in Wales, the Lakes and now Scotland. The creation of the Wednesday Section and regular mid week climbing meets assisted in giving members further opportunity to enjoy the essence of our Club, the fellowship of the hills.

Kinder Scout near Red Brook. *Photo by J. Beatty*

In July 1982, Rob Ferguson, Ted Courtenay, John Beatty and member in waiting Robin Illingworth took 44 days to man-haul sledges across the central ice cap of Greenland in celebration of Nansen's first crossing.
Photo by J. Beatty

The halfway point at Kidhow Gate during an unsuccessful Pennine Way record attempt. *Left to right.* Mike Cudahy, Chris Bolshaw, Mark Cudahy, John Richardson, Geoff Bell. *Photo by J. Beatty*

Brian Cosby completed all the Alpine four thousand metre peaks.
Photo by B. Cosby

1980   A year for America. Dave Cowans and Mike Ryan enjoyed The Nose, El Capitan. • Half Dome is climbed by Mike Ryan on the Direct Route and by Cec Rhodes and Don Cowans on the NW Face.

1981   Tim Leach climbed the North Pillar of Rooster Comb, West Face of Mount Huntingdon and the West Buttress of Mount McKinley, and reached an unclimbed pinnacle on Annapurna III at 6705m. • The Sinclairs go pot-holing in Spain, joining a team from Derbyshire Caving Club and Italian Alpine Club. They became the first British team to bottom the Cima G.E.S.M., then the fifth deepest cave in the world at -1800m. • The Easter Meet at Cluanie Lodge had quite remarkable weather, four days brilliantly sunny and hot. • Despite his previous comments, Geoff Bell repeats a solo self-supported Pennine Way. (Taking 4 days, 22 hours and 49 minutes).

1982   Ted Courtenay, John Beatty and Rob Ferguson were half the party repeating Nansen's epic crossing of Greenland. • Brian Cosby completed the Alpine 4000m summits.

1983   The Island Meet on Coll was prolonged due to gales. • The Alpine Meets were revived, Ailefroid the venue. • Walter Riley's 80th birthday was celebrated by his climbing on the Milestone Buttress, champagne atop Tryfan and a feast at Beudy Mawr. • Don Cowans was tragically killed whilst winter climbing on Crib y Ddysgl.

1984   Mike Cudahy set a new record by traversing the Pennine Way in under three days, (on foot). • Neil Mather completed the Tranter Round, (Glen Nevis circuit).

Dave Cowans *pictured*, and Mike Ryan climb the Nose of El Capitan. 1980.
Photo by M. Ryan

In 1986 Tony Ryan climbed Rubicon, Britain's first 8a+. Water cum Jolly.
Photo by Steve Lewis

Peter Roberts followed in the Club's traditions of legendary Hut Wardens with his dedicated service as warden of Beudy Mawr for 23 years. This has not deterred him from his love of wild places. He has now completed the round of the Munros three times and in his retirement he can in any one year be found in Greenland, Antarctica, Svalbard – to name but a few.

Eddie Thurrell, *left*, competed in the Three Peaks Yacht Race in 1987. After 400 nautical miles and 73 land miles, the team finished 12th overall.

Ron Fawcett (member from 1990-97) climbing Edge Lane E3 at Millstone Edge. *Photo by J. Beatty*

George Hostford and sister Jo climbed the Cassin Route on Piz Badile during the Club's Alpine Meet, 1986. *Photo by Jo Hostford.*

1985 Ian Tattersall successfully climbed the Lotus Flower Tower in the Yukon, and had an epic descent. • Alistair Macdonald produced a TV programme "Two by Two", covering the Karrimor Mountain Marathon. Mike Cudahy and John Richardson figured prominently, with glimpses of seven other Club members. • Arthur Clarke became the Superveteran Welsh Fell Running Champion.

1986 The Welsh Classical Round, The Paddy Buckley Round, tackled by Chris Bolshaw, Eddie Thurrell, in less than 24 hours, and John Crummett to become the 5th, 6th and 7th to complete the Round. • Bill Deakin and Phil Thompson made a 3 day ascent of The Nose, El Capitan, Yosemite. • John Richardson ran and cycled The Three Peaks - Snowdon, Scafell, Ben Nevis, 430 miles cycled, 10-11 thousand feet ascended, during appallingly bad weather, in 58 hours including stops. • Peter Roberts completed his second tour of the Munros. • Ian Tattersall climbed Mera by the south face, Khumbu Himalaya. • George Hostford with his sister Jo climbed the Cassin Route on the Piz Badile during the Alpine meet. • The Island Meet failed to reach Eigg, expected hurricane force winds caused the boat to remain tied to its pier. The meet retired to Arisaig Youth Hostel. • Philip Brockbank and Herbert Hartley died.

1987 Eddie Thurrell joined a team on the Three Peaks Yacht Race. • Rob Ferguson was again in Greenland, making the third ascent of the Arctic and Greenland's highest mountain, Gunnbjornsfeld, 4001m. • In May, the Tan-Cat walk of 120 miles took 55 hours. • The London Section celebrated their Golden Jubilee, Keith Treacher published its history, "The Gentlemen of London".

The Club's London Section celebrated their Golden Jubilee in 1987. *Left to right*, John Richardson, Brian Rhodes (hidden), Ken Pearson, John Lee, Taffy Davies, Peter Greenaway, Frank Solari, John Hepworth, Ted Courtenay, Sue Richardson, Harry Law, John Whyte.

Ian Tattersall experienced incidents during an attempt on the south side of Annapurna III. • Inken Blunk planned an extended Scottish Fours taking in assorted extra Munros and to finish over Mount Keen. With Mike Cudahy most of the route was covered, but very sore feet prevented the finish over Lochnagar and Mount Keen. • The Meets Programme was very full - a meet was held nearly every weekend and covered climbing, walking, fell running, canoeing, cycling, camping, bothying and iglooing. • Long walks included the Lake District Top Twenty and the Grassington-Langdale. • Members were active in Nepal, New Zealand, Peru, USA, Morocco and Antarctica.

The North Wales Horseshoe took John Richardson, Wade Cooper, John Crummett, Chris Bolshaw, Andy Howie and Eddie Thurrell 64 hours 57 minutes to cover the 135 miles. Inken Blunk covered 110 miles, including 6 hours during the second night navigating difficult country solo. • Following a suggestion from Ted Dance at the A.G.M., a "Wednesday Group" composed of those members and friends able to spend the weekday enjoying pleasant walks came into being. • Noel Kirkman received the O.B.E. for services to Mountain Rescue.

Inken Blunk route planning with Mike Cudahy. Inken is the Club's leading long distance female athlete having made several walks over a hundred miles. *Photo by J. Beatty*

Chris and Gill Bolshaw viewing Stac an Armin in the St Kilda group during a Scottish Island Meet that attracted 12 members to make the 57 mile sea crossing. *Photo by J. Beatty*

A memorable Scottish Island Meet on Colonsay. Standing around the fire *left to right*, are, Courtenay, Dillon, Andy Llewellyn, Gordon Adshead. *Photo by J. Beatty*

Scottish Island Meet on Rhum at Dibidil bothy.

Keith Treacher, author of "Siegfried Herford – An Edwardian Rock Climber", is a great upholder of the traditions of the Club. The current Secretary remembers being roundly ticked off for publishing the occupation of a newly elected member in Meetstaff – "Once you're a Rucksacker, that's all that matters". He has been an imaginative and ingenious leader of Club Meets, at many of which the après montagne activities have been totally memorable. *Photo by J. T. H. Allen*

Ted Courtenay sledge hauling in the coastal mountains of Kronprins Frederik Mountains. 1990.

Dave Woolley looking out over dozens of unclimbed peaks in the remote Kronprins Frederik Mountains of East Greenland. Other members of the Northern Group Expedition were Rob Ferguson, Ted Courtenay, Ian Campbell and John Richardson. 1990. *Photo by R. Ferguson.*

From left to right, Dave Sinclair, Rob Ferguson and Stephen Sinclair, with Rod Mumford and John Heginbotham descended the one thousand metre cave system of Fuente de Escuain in a continuous 26 hour epic in the Pyrenees. 1991. *Photo by R. Mumford*

Bill Deakin and Cec Rhodes made a successful ascent of the Eiger North Face in 1990. Bill Deakin *pictured* is crossing the infamous Hinterstoisser Traverse. *Photo by Cec Rhodes*

1990 Bill Deakin and Cec Rhodes climbed the Eiger by the North Face. • Peter Cockshott completed the Tranter Round. • Club members formed over half the Northern Group East Greenland Expedition. • Ten first ascents were made during exploration of the Kronsprins Frederik Mountains. • Frank Williamson, Alec Ferguson and Al Cowburn died. • At an E.G.M. in September a motion to allow women to become members was carried by the narrowest of margins. The Treasurer then looked forward to collecting subs. from a number of persons hitherto being beyond his grasp. • Mike Cudahy led an enterprising and new walk, "The High Watermarks of the Lake District" - twenty one named tarns visited, about 60 miles, "A good walk worth repeating". • Mike and Don Talbot did the Welsh Threes, the Lakes Threes and the Scottish Fours including the Greater Traverse, cycling in between the areas. • Mike Hartley covered the Ramsey Round, the Bob Graham Round and the Paddy Buckley Round in 3 days, 14 hours and 20 minutes which included 7 hours 40 minutes travel by car between the Rounds. • Vin Dillon led his 31th and final "High Camp" on Cader Idris.

1991 Douglas Milner, Jack Cooper, Cyril Wickham, Jack Caldwell, Alfred Williamson, Len Kiernan, Peter Wild, Vernon Chapman and Taffy Davies died - in no other year has the Club lost so many notable members. • New lady members led excellent and well-attended meets - Jean Llewellyn organised a notable weekend in Buttermere, Inken Blunk led the longest walk in the year's programme - 90 miles Armathwaite to Settle, and Carole Smithies took over the High Camp meets with a camp appropriately on Scafell Pike. • Clive Morton and Keith Hodgkinson enjoyed the Cassin Route on the North Wall of the Piz Badile in preparation for a damp ascent of the Walker Spur.

Bill Deakin Eigerwandering.1990.
Photo by Cec Rhodes.

1992 The Devil's Tower, Wyoming, gave Gary Ryan and Martin Wills an enjoyable climb. • Joe Kyle and Mike Cudahy did well on "The Dragon's Back", the first U.K. Multi-day Mountain Marathon, Conway to Carreg Cennen Castle, Swansea. • The Committee agreed in principle to sell the Library. • John Crummett completed the Scottish Fours solo, without support, in under 35 hours despite poor weather. • Peter Harding managed 235 climbs in the year. • Mike Ryan captained the British Sport Climbing Team and was the highest placed British competitor in the Final. • Our oldest member, Bernard Meldrum, died aged 107. He had been on the second ascent of Central Buttress, Scafell.

1993 Craigallan was bought, the Library was withdrawn from Manchester Central Library and Arthur Clarke presented a detailed report on the condition of High Moss and the work required to re-fit this hut. • Rob Ferguson was joined by Jim Lowther, Chris Bonington and Graham Little in a feast of first ascenting in East Greenland. • Peter Harding soloed the Matterhorn in his 70th year. • Bill Deakin added the Bob Graham Round to his belt which already held an ascent of the Eiger North Wall. • Dave and Eunice Sinclair walked from Corinth to Albania, very enjoyable except for nasty encounters with ferocious dogs. • North America continued to attract the climbers, whilst the Goldsmiths walked and climbed in South Africa.

Dave Williams on the first true English ascent of
Pacific Ocean Wall in Yosemite. 1982

Alf Gleadell climbed Salathé Wall. Yosemite.1986.

Rob Ferguson joined an expedition to the Lemonsberg Mountains of East Greenland with Chris Bonington, Graham Little and Jim Lowther. Little *pictured* is climbing the final pitch to the summit of The Chisel, 1993.
Photo by R. Ferguson.

Roger Booth at the opening ceremony of Craigallan. As Hut Warden, Roger inspired and supervised the whole refurbishment project. *Photo by Mike Dent*

Craigallan Hut, Ballachulish.
Photo by Mike Dent

Gerry Goldsmith reached 7,400m on Tirich Mir 7,707m
the highest peak of the Hindu Kush, 1995.

Mike Ryan, Dave Sinclair, Shelagh
Moore, Dave Cowans and John
Warburton. *Photo Mike Ryan Collection*

Ian Tattersall *right* with Joe Simpson *left*, climbed Alpamayo in Peru.1995. *Photo by J. Simpson*

Dave Williams on New Dawn, El Capitan, Yosemite.

1994 An active year, commencing with excellent weather, fine and frosty, for the Marsden to Edale, with Geoff Bell and John Crummett completing a "Double-double". (6.10 am Friday to 4.30pm Saturday). • Mike Cudahy made a continuous traverse on foot of the Munros in under 67 days. • Septuagenarians were in particularly good form: Ron Whitehead climbed Dream of White Horses, Peter Harding repeated Promontory Traverse at Black Rocks - he being the first ascencionist forty years previously - and in the Alps he soloed the Youngrat on the Breithorn. • Keith Treacher completed the 2000 feet summits of Ted Moss's list. • Members worked energetically on Craigallan - the bunks were prefabricated in Scarborough by Pauls Riley and Shearman. • The sale of the Library raised an immediate £37,000.

1995 Craigallan was officially opened on 24th June by the President, Ted Dance. • The weather was glorious. • Members were active far and wide. • Neil and Gerry Goldsmith were on a successful expedition to Tirich Mir. • Deakin trekked and climbed in the Karakoram, Bill then climbed Batian and Nelion on Mount Kenya. • Others were active in the New World where Dave Williams spent a memorable nine days on an ascent of New Dawn on El Capitan. (One day was spent sitting out a snow storm on a porta-ledge, the food ran out on the last two). • Ian Tattersall with Joe Simpson climbed Alpamayo. • In addition to a local walk each and every week of the year the Wednesday Club held meets at High Moss, Braemar, Skye and Corsica. • The changing social scene was evidenced by a Disco following the Annual Dinner and a Ceilidh replacing the December Hot Pot Supper. • Ken Davidson and Noel Kirkman OBE died.

1996 A major refurbishment of Beudy Mawr took place.
• Club members maintained a very high level of
activity both on Club meets and otherwise with
teams operating in Africa, the Americas, Asia, the
Alps, the Dolomites and Spain. • Ron Whitehead, 77,
stood atop the Old Man of Hoy. • John Richardson
and Mike Cudahy completed the Three Peaks,
Snowdon - Scafell Pike - Ben Nevis on foot and cycle
in 56 hours. • Five members completed the Munros.
• Amongst memorable meets was the Marsden - Edale
with a record eighty participants. Unfortunately
dense mist throughout the day resulted in many
small groups rarely if ever meeting. • The Meet of the
Year for those lucky enough to be present was Jo
Carter's "Kidnapped" based on David Balfour's
wanderings through Mull and Ardgour. • Joint meets
with the M.U.M.C. restarted after a gap of many
years. • Frank Solari and Ivan Waller died.

A classic meet of the year was Jo Carter's 'Kidnapped'
meet, based on the wanderings of David Balfour round
Mull and Ardgour.
Photo by G. Goldsmith

1997 Paul Murray, youthful 55 years old, covered 55
Lakeland tops in 23 hours 24 minutes. • Ted Dance
and Tom Gerrard showed that youthful zest can last
beyond retirement: in 4 weeks they managed to
include 10 Alpine 4000 metre summits amongst their
activities. • In Yosemite Dave Williams and Bill
Deakin climbed Salathé Wall and also on El Cap the
Ryan brothers Tony and Gary rapidly climbed Zodiac
whilst others enjoyed day routes in the Valley. • The
Wednesday Club only managed to walk on 52
occasions in a year of 53 Wednesdays, but made up
for it with climbing trips to the Costa Blanca and
exploring the Queras • The Island Meet gave Barra a
second chance and members were rewarded with
excellent weather and an enormous "howff" - the
Island's spacious and excellently appointed Sports
Centre.

Brian Cosby *left,*and John Richardson make
a continuous traverse of the Haute Route.
Photo by J. Richardson

The annual Club walk from Marsden to Edale was well attended in 1996 with eighty participants. Conditions were atrocious with thick mist and driving rain.
Photo by J. Beatty

In the High Peak Marathon 1998, the Rucksack Club scored highly with three teams making the honours. *Left to right*, John Crummett, Geoff Bell, Wade Cooper, John Richardson, Liam Cudahy, Mark Cudahy, Gerard Cudahy, Derek Clutterbuck, Charlotte Roberts, Dave Woolley and Jo Kyle.

Lundy Meet 2000.

Mike and Gary Ryan on top of Moonlight Buttress in Zion National Park, Utah. *Photo by Mike Ryan*

Gary Ryan on Moonlight Buttress. Zion, Utah.
Photo by Mike Ryan

Over 100 members, their families and friends celebrated simultaneously the 30th anniversary of High Moss and the 95th birthday of Walter Riley. Honorary Member Walter's professional skill and enthusiasm has been a feature of every one of the Club huts, shown here recieving a cake from Jean Llewellyn.

Geoff Bell cycles from John o' Groats to Land's End and traverses Ben Nevis, Scafell and Snowdon en route, all in 8 days.
Photo by Mike Cudahy

Geoff Bell on the summit of Ben Nevis in May, during his long ride. *Photo by G. Bell*

1998 Tom Gerrard climbs the NE face of Piz Badile with Jim Hall. • February - Beudy Mawr 50th Anniversary Meet attended, amongst many others, by 3 members who had been present at the first ever Beudy meet - Peter Roberts, Arthur Bullough and Albert Dale. • May – 15 members of the "Wednesday Club" mount a successful assault on the Irish "3s" June – 107 members and guests celebrate Walter Riley's 95th birthday and High Moss's 30th • Rucksack Club teams win all three trophies in the High Peak Marathon. • John Crummett and Geoff Bell complete the Joss Naylor Challenge. • Peter Roberts uses his retirement well, climbing in Greenland and South Georgia. • Gerry Goldsmith climbs Khantengri (7000m) in the Tien Shan. • Alistair Macdonald was a member of the Lowe's Gully Expedition (Borneo). • September – Trevor Hart completes the Cambrian Way, suffering gales and rainstorms on the way.

1999 Brian Cosby celebrates 65th birthday by walking from Ben Nevis to Snowdon via Scafell, using RC and F&RCC huts on the way. • Geoff Bell, Pete Neumann and Gerry Goldsmith complete the Paris-Brest-Paris cycle ride in under 90 hours. • RC teams win the Fellsman Race and two trophies in the High Peak Marathon. • Gordon Adshead and Tom Anderson complete their bags of Corbetts, and Don Smithies passes the 1,000 mark of Marilyns climbed. • Mike and Gary Ryan, and Andy Stewart active on American big walls. • Ian Tattersall dies in a parapente accident.

2000 Three of our oldest members died: Frank Kiernan, Frank Bennett and Arthur Bullough, all well over 90 years old, also Ted Courtenay. • Keith Treacher publishes his Biography of Siegfried Herford. • Geoff Bell rides from Land's End to John o' Groats via Snowdon, Scafell and Ben Nevis in 8 days, staying at the Club huts on the way. • Andy Stewart solos The Nose in mixed weather. • Gordon Adshead leads his last Igloo Meet on Ben Nevis in superb conditions. • Rob Ferguson returned to South Greenland with Chris Bonington to make first ascents of several fine peaks.

Mike Ferguson *back left* leading one of the Club's increasingly popular cycling meets, on this occasion, to traverse the Lakeland high passes. *Photo by Gerry Goldsmith*

2001 Foot and mouth epidemic causes the Club huts to be closed for varying periods and the Outdoor Programme is curtailed. Much ingenuity by leaders in arranging substitutes for advertised meets. • Peter Roberts (age 70+) climbing in Antarctica and Greenland, Roger Booth joins a party completing the "Shackleton Crossing" of South Georgia. • Alex Miller reports on ski touring in Iran. • Brian Cosby and son-in-law complete a centenary celebration ascent of Observatory Ridge on Ben Nevis.

2002 Centenary Year. John Richardson, grandson of co-founder John Entwisle elected President. • Tan-Cat and Barmouth-Aber revisited. • A wine and cheese party meet on Laddow with some attempts at Edwardian costume. • President leads highly successful triathlon meet based on Beudy Mawr. Relay teams complete the Eustace Thomas Classic Lakeland Round. • Don Smithies leads "Welsh 3,000s with Dignity", a 3 day trip involving stays at the club's historical huts – Cwm Eigiau, Tal y Braich and Beudy Mawr. • Joint meets held with the Gritstone, Pinnacle and the Fell and Rock Clubs, 300 members and guests celebrate the Rucksack Club Centenary with a Dinner in Manchester Town Hall on 12th October.

Ron Whitehead at 79, *left*, with Cec Rhodes *right* climbing the East Arête of Cima Grande. *Photo by W. Deakin*

Bill Deakin *pictured*, and Mike Ryan climbed Mescalito on El Capitan over six days in September 2001.
Photo by M. Ryan

Members gathered at Laddow Rocks to celebrate the spirit of the early Rucksack pioneers. Here, Carole Smithies (the Club's first lady member) climbing in period costume.
Photo by Mike Dent

A. O. 'TAFFY' DAVIES
1944-1991
The king of involuntary bivouacs.

"Oh, may my heart's song still be sung
On this high hill
In a year's turning."
Dylan Thomas